Silk Road Research Series

Series Editor

Xiao Li, Renmin University of China, Beijing, China

Since the international development strategy known as "Belt and Road" was officially proposed by Chinese President Xi Jinping in 2013, the field of Silk Road studies has attracted renewed attention around the globe. Springer Nature, together with the SDX Joint Publishing Company, has built upon this development with their new academic publication, the Silk Road Research Series (SRRS).

As a high-level, interdisciplinary academic platform, the Series will provide both established academics and ambitious early-career researchers an opportunity to present their work. While a considerable part of the research related to the Silk Road is being pursued in China and being published in Chinese, we consider it vital to encourage and assist Chinese experts with publishing their research results in English and in a Western style in the Series.

As a new conceptual approach, the focus of SRRS will not only be on the historical, extensive Silk Road trade network that connected the Eurasian civilizations in the distant past; it will also shed light on the contemporary political and economic dynamics that shape the new Silk Road. The content will cover a broad spectrum of fields, including history, archaeology, linguistics, religious studies, geography, art and economics from prehistoric to modern times, and ranging from the Mediterranean and Egypt to Western and Central Asia and China.

Xiao Li
Editor

Major Archaeological Discoveries Along the Chinese Silk Road

Editor
Xiao Li
Renmin University of China
Beijing, China

ISSN 2524-390X   ISSN 2524-3918 (electronic)
Silk Road Research Series
ISBN 978-981-99-0661-1   ISBN 978-981-99-0659-8 (eBook)
https://doi.org/10.1007/978-981-99-0659-8

Jointly published with SDX Joint Publishing
The print edition is not for sale in China (Mainland). Customers from China (Mainland) please order the print book from: SDX Joint Publishing.

© SDX Joint Publishing 2023
This work is subject to copyright. All rights are reserved by the Publisher, whether the whole or part of the material is concerned, specifically the rights of translation, reprinting, reuse of illustrations, recitation, broadcasting, reproduction on microfilms or in any other physical way, and transmission or information storage and retrieval, electronic adaptation, computer software, or by similar or dissimilar methodology now known or hereafter developed.
The use of general descriptive names, registered names, trademarks, service marks, etc. in this publication does not imply, even in the absence of a specific statement, that such names are exempt from the relevant protective laws and regulations and therefore free for general use.
The publisher, the authors and the editors are safe to assume that the advice and information in this book are believed to be true and accurate at the date of publication. Neither the publisher nor the authors or the editors give a warranty, express or implied, with respect to the material contained herein or for any errors or omissions that may have been made. The publisher remains neutral with regard to jurisdictional claims in published maps and institutional affiliations.

This Springer imprint is published by the registered company Springer Nature Singapore Pte Ltd.
The registered company address is: 152 Beach Road, #21-01/04 Gateway East, Singapore 189721, Singapore

Editorial Advisory Board

Prof. Nicholas Sims-Williams, SOAS University of London
Prof. Jianjun Mei, The Needham Research Institute
Prof. Mayke Wagner, German Archaeological Institute, Eurasia Department
Prof. Abdurishid Yakup, Berlin-Brandenburg Academy of Sciences and Humanities
Prof. Etienne de la Vaissiere, Ecole des Hautes Etudes en Sciences Sociales
Prof. Irina Popova, Institute of Oriental Manuscripts, Russian Academy of Sciences
Prof. Sergei Miniaev, Institute of the History of Material Culture of the Russian Academy of Sciences
Assoc. Prof. Dr. Cengiz Alyimaz, Ataturk University Kazim Karabekir Education Faculty Department of Turkish Language Teaching Yoncalik
Prof. Mehmet Oelmez Yildiz, Turkey Teknik University
Prof. Dr. M. B. Vosoughi, History Department, Tehran University, Iran
Prof. Ismailova Jannat Khamidovna, State Museum of the History of Uzbekistan Doctor of Historical Sciences
Prof. Yoshida Yutaka, Graduate School of Letters, Kyoto University, Japan
Prof. Valerie Hansen, Yale University
Prof. Xinjiang Rong, Peking University
Prof. Yuqi Zhu, Peking University
Prof. Qing Duan, Peking University
Prof. Yu Zhang, School of Economics Renmin University of China
Prof. Xianshi Meng, School of Chinese Classics of Renmin University of China
Prof. Wuyun·Bilig, School of Chinese Classics of Renmin University of China
Prof. Weirong Shen, School of Chinese Classics of Renmin University of China
Prof. Bo Bi, School of Chinese Classics of Renmin University of China
Prof. Yugui Wu, History Institute of Chinese Academy of Social Sciences
Prof. Chongxin Yao, Department of Anthropology at Sun Yat-sen University
Prof. Feng Zhao, China National Silk Museum
Prof. Feng Luo, Ningxia Institute of Archaeology
Dir. Dongqiang Er, Shanghai Er Dongqiang Silk Road Vision Literature Centre
Prof. Defang Zhang, Gansu Bamboo Slips Museum

Preface of Silk Road Research Series

In recent years, conducting research on the Silk Road has become a popular trend in the international academia. Without a doubt, this is directly related to China's Belt and Road initiative. At the same time, we notice that this particular trend is also a reflection on how the academia in the East and the West leverage the topic and engage in dialogue. Furthermore, this represents efforts by scholars in the post-Cold War world to promote direct dialogue on issues that are of common interest, rather talking past each other.

There are two senses about the Silk Road. The narrow sense is about economic and cultural exchanges between ancient China and countries in Central Asia, South Asia, West Asia, and the Mediterranean region. On the other hand, the broad sense refers to all kinds of exchanges between the East and the West. As such, understanding of the Silk Road in the academia has long been tilted towards the popular narrative, and a majority of Silk Road research, in fact, caters to the taste of the general public.

Nevertheless, the Silk Road epitomizes all kinds of exchanges of material and spiritual cultures across a vast area, from China to Rome, and from the equator to the North Pole.

As such, the development of Eastern and Western civilizations and their interactions in Asia and Europe can be understood within the Silk Road framework. In this vein, many far-sighted scholars have long ago started making use of this broad concept to consolidate the many common points emerged from a variety of academic research. This also leads to the emergence of many issues that are of interest to both the East and the West. In particular, the many archaeological relics unearthed at old Silk Road towns have become the focal points in Silk Road research, as these relics exemplify the intermixture of Eastern and Western civilizations. Silk Road towns like Chang'an, Dunhuang, Turpan, Bamiyan, Ai-Khanum, Samarkand, and Palmyra have attracted the attention of scholars, and the related Silk Road research is also linked to a wide variety of disciplines, such as archaeology, history, Dunhuang Studies, Iranian studies, and classical studies.

Over the years, there have been many scholarly works on the Silk Road. Yet, on its own, Silk Road is not an official academic discipline. Therefore, the relevant research results are classified under the related disciplines. In China, they are often seen through the lens of history of Chinese-Western communications, history of Sino-foreign relations or history of cultural exchange between China and the world. That said, we understand that a stringent Silk Road research requires a scholarly journal about the Silk Road.

In the past, due to the popularization of concepts relating to the Silk Road, most magazines dealing with the topic were focused on content that were of popular interest. In fact, only a few titles were scholarly in nature. In the early 1990s, *Silk Road Art and Archaeology*, a journal published by the Institute of Silk Road Studies, which was in turn founded by Ikuo Hirayama, played an active role in advancing scholarly research on the Silk Road. Unfortunately, the passing away of Ikuo Hirayama had dealt a severe blow to the journal, as it was unable to continue operation. On the other hand, *The Silk Road*, supported solely by American scholar Prof. Daniel C. Waugh since 2000, has also become unsustainable despite its rich content.

Fortunately, under China's Belt and Road initiative, the academia and publishers in China have shown a great deal of interest in Silk Road research. Within the past two to three years, we have seen the birth of numerous scholarly journals bearing the "Silk Road" name. Among them is *Silk Road Research Series*, a large-scale and comprehensive scholarly journal edited by Li Xiao and published by Sanlian Bookstore. The first volume, in Chinese, has already been published, and it deals with wide-ranging subject matters, such as archaeology, history, the arts, language, religion, and culture.

Now, we are launching the English version of *Silk Road Research Series,* and the content is sourced from the Chinese version as well as fresh contributions. The majority of the authors in the English version are Chinese scholars, and in some senses, this represents the contributions of Chinese authors to this field of study. We also hope that we can engage in dialogue with our international counterparts through this medium to advance research on the Silk Road. As the mother tongue of the authors and editors is not English, it is a challenge for them to publicize their works in this language. We hope that through our concerted efforts, this English-language journal will be more refined in the not-so-distant future.

Beijing, China   Xinjiang Rong

Foreword: Prospect and Retrospect

In June of this year, Professor Li Xiao asked me to write a preface for his edited book *The Studies of Silk Road*, and I was really frightened and nervous, thus I kept putting it off. I have the impression that writing a preface to a scholar's work is a matter of friendship, but more often, it is a sublime from a sophisticated scholar. As far as I am concerned, the former may be compatible, while the latter I might not be qualified. However, since I have agreed to do so, I have to complete this preface, which is not in a style of preface, as a contribution to my friend Li Xiao's academic project.

Since the 1980s, the archaeology, history, geography, and other disciplines associated with the Silk Road have become prominent in China, and the academic works sprung up. Even the academic achievements related to archaeology have been impressive. It can be said that the development of archaeology and the depth of research results have played a key role in enriching the study of the Silk Road.

The archaeology of the Silk Road in China is based on the archaeology of Western and frontier provinces (regions) of China (the field of study also includes adjacent countries). Due to the specificity of these regions, the archaeology of the Silk Road is both intrinsic to the construction of the discipline and problem-oriented, both of which need to be balanced. From the point of view of academic research, this concept is both historical and dynamic, and its field of study is also characterized by international and regional exchanges, so that the content of research is also international; along with the emergence of sound theories, materials, and new tools, the discipline is becoming increasingly mature; with new materials, new results, and new understanding as the main features of the "Silk Road" archaeology, we promote our understanding of the ancient interaction. In this way, Silk Road archaeology increasingly become the core of today's academic area and gradually become one of the popular subdisciplines of Chinese archaeology.

The "Silk Road" was first mentioned only in relation to the Han Dynasty in Chinese history and as a single silk trade route. Since the late 19th century, it has become synonymous with cultural exchanges between East and West, with an increasingly broad connotation. As far as archaeology is concerned, it includes all phases from the Palaeolithic Period to the Tang and Song dynasties, with many archaeological projects containing the Neolithic, Bronze Age, and historical periods, and covering a wide range of topics. In terms of form, most projects are based on archaeological research, while combining with various new scientific and technological means, historical documents, and carrying out holistic multidisciplinary research to extract the maximum amount of information to achieve good results, where this has become the most important aspect of academic achievements in the development of Chinese archaeology over the past century. In terms of theoretical construction achieved by the discipline of frontier archaeology, the outcomes and research history of frontier archaeology have begun to be sorted out. In terms of methodology, the archaeology, ethnicity, and religion of the frontier region have been incorporated into the research horizon to seek the way of historical truth. In particular, the study of the archaeology of the Han and Tang dynasties is more problem-oriented, highlighting the central government's jurisdiction and governance of the border areas and the process of cultural exchange between the mainland and the border areas during and after the Han and Tang dynasties, and conducting a comprehensive archaeological study of ancient city sites, relics along the Silk Road and Buddhist sites during the Han and Tang dynasties. It will show the process of social identification at the border areas (all ethnic groups) with the Chinese family and deepen the understanding of the diversity in uniformity of Chinese civilization.

Studies have shown that the archaeology of the Silk Road is becoming more and more advanced, involving the basic theory of archaeological disciplines, the identification and interaction of archaeological cultures, ancient environment and biology, physical anthropology and DNA genetic research, flora and fauna, metallurgical history, and other aspects.

All of this can be seen as a multifaceted and multi-angle exploration and description of the social development in the prehistoric and historical periods touched by the archaeology of the Silk Road. Although the depth and breadth of these studies are not as complete as they could be and may not have reached the point of accurately tracing the prehistoric societies in this region, the researchers have begun to pry or are resolving the obstacles that lie in the way of exploration, and thus, the future is promising.

The basic features of Palaeolithic and Neolithic archaeological cultures in the archaeology of the Silk Road have always been a matter of concern for scholars. Although the accurate dating of these sites and the stratigraphic problems still limit the researchers to study these remains in depth, the exploration never stops. In the study of Bronze Age archaeological culture, although the focus has been "coincidentally" on the zoning and staging of Bronze Age archaeological culture in Xinjiang, which is not only a requirement of the development stage of research but also indicates the importance of this topic in the construction of the framework of archaeological culture in Xinjiang, we have made great advancement. The research design from the perspective of natural science in recent years has covered such important topics as the archaeological early metallurgical development of the Silk Road and its relationship with the surrounding areas, which is also an important element in archaeological research. The application of natural science and technology in archaeology has also opened up some new research fields and expanded the research horizon. The maturation of technologies such as starch granules, plant microsomes, and diet analysis has promoted new progress in the field of plant and animal archaeology on the Silk Road, including some very important topics, such as the spread of wheat in Xinjiang and the emergence of domestic horses.

The study of ancient races in the Xinjiang region has been the exclusive domain of Western researchers for a long time, since 1929, when A. Keith published his study of skull data from burials in the northeastern Taklamakan Desert. In the context of the increasing research in Chinese archaeology and bioanthropology, the use of human mitochondrial DNA genetic data and the use of molecular genetic methods to study the ethnography of the ancient inhabitants around the Silk Road began to take off, which has attracted a great attention.

Based on the continuous discovery of new materials, research has also been carried out in depth, with the following main features:

The first aspect is manifested in a new stage in the construction of archaeological disciplines. On top of the accumulation of abundant materials, scholars have become more and more comprehensive in their understanding and consideration of the archaeological framework of prehistory (Bronze Age) in Xinjiang. Based on a series of studies, Chen Ge (陈戈) successively developed his research of the prehistoric period ("Silk Road") in Xinjiang, dividing the prehistoric culture before Han into clear references to the Palaeolithic, Mesolithic, Neolithic, Chalcolithic Age, Bronze Age, and Early Iron Age; Shui Tao (水涛 1993) divided the prehistoric (mainly Bronze Age) remains in Xinjiang into eight regions and comprehensively and systematically summarized and analysed the prehistoric cultural pattern in Xinjiang; An Zhimin (安志敏1996) proposed that the Tarim Basin be the centre and divided the area centred on the Tarim Basin into ten cultural sub-regions and pointed out the differences among the regions. Han Jianye (韩建业2005) proposed the concept of staging and genealogy of Bronze Age-Early Iron Age cultures in Xinjiang, and divided ten sub-regions, and discussed the cultural nature of the above-mentioned remains and their connection with the surrounding area; Guo Wu (郭物 2012)'s discussion of the interrelationships of prehistoric cultures in Xinjiang and their connections with the outside world is particularly in-depth. Shao Huiqiu (邵会秋), Liu Xuedang (刘学堂), Ruan Qiurong (阮秋荣), and Jia Weiming (贾伟明) Cong Dexin (丛德新) also contributed in the discussion. With the fully consideration, the study is characterized by an increasingly detailed analysis of the construction forms of the remains, burial customs and other elements which is based on the study of pottery assemblages and other accompanying burial objects.

The second aspect is the increasing depth of research on cultural origins (East-West cultural exchange), social development, and subsistence patterns. These researches are also one of the foundations of the archaeological study of the Bronze Age "Silk Road" in Xinjiang. Li Shuicheng (李水城 2005) conducted an in-depth study on the prehistoric cultural links between eastern Xinjiang and the Ganqing region, arguing that both eastern Xinjiang and the Ganqing region were important channels for the spread of early bronze smelting technique and cultural exchanges between the East and the West, as well as intermediary areas linking the Yellow River and Central Asian civilizations. Gong Guoqiang (龚国强 1997) discussed the unearthed and collected artefacts such as mirrors with handles, square plates, and bronze Fu (鍑) in the Yili Valley, pointing out their similarity in morphology and age to the remains of the Saka culture in the Seven Rivers Valley of Central Asia and the Tagar culture in South Siberia. Lin Yun (林沄 2008) pointed out that the Chemurchek type is from a different tradition of archaeological culture from the Afanasyevo and Andronovo cultures, and that the influence of Chemurchek on Bronze Age archaeological culture in Xinjiang was widespread, even to the south of the Tianshan Mountains and to the East of Xinjiang.

In recent years, along with the diversity of archaeological data and the depth of research, scholars have increasingly focused on the social development and subsistence patterns of the Bronze Age in the Xinjiang region. In a series of papers published by Wang Jianxin (王建新), Cong Dexin, and Jia Weiming, the level of development of animal husbandry is discussed, and the early nomadic mode of this period-the seasonal (cyclical) transhumance of crowds and the possibility of its existence are explored as well.

The third area of progress is that multidisciplinary research has become broader and deeper, with achievements in bioanthropology, ancient DNA research, and research on plants, animals, and various organic matter artefacts; research on plant flotation and plant microsomes, as well as research on the date of the emergence of wheat, corn, and millet, and the routes of dissemination, are also gaining new results.

The fourth part is the increasingly widespread practice of new concepts in archaeology and the rapid progress in the application of new technologies due to technological advances. In the last decade, various new technologies, such as aerial photography and remote sensing, have been applied to archaeological practice more and more commonly. These include the widely accepted concepts of GIS and landscape archaeology, which have also provided new means and ways of understanding the archaeological study of the Silk Road.

Finally, two points I believe that in future "Silk Road" archaeology should also focus on:

First, we should focus on the study of the archaeological culture of the "Silk Road" around the Tarim Basin. The Tarim Basin should be considered as a closely related cultural unit, and the study and understanding of archaeological culture and interaction in the region is an important part of the archaeological study of the Silk Road in Xinjiang. At present, the exploration of early Bronze Age archaeological cultures study in the marginal region of the Tarim Basin is still in its initial stage. At the same time, further exploration of other areas around the Tarim Basin and the establishment of a unified standard for distinguishing different types of archaeology are still to be further explored. It is believed that a deeper understanding of the remains around the Tarim Basin will provide further reliable background information for the understanding of the ancient Chinese texts, such as the *Records of the History* and the *Book of Han*, about the Western states and the basic aspects of the prehistoric Xinjiang region.

We should pay attention to the study on the relationship between prehistoric archaeological culture and the "Silk Road". Xinjiang is located in the key crux where the cultural exchanges between China and the West took place, the in-depth study of early archaeological culture in Xinjiang, for the interpretation of the origin, development, and specific connotations of the "Silk Road", have a fundamental role. Compared with the relatively abundant archaeological research on the Silk Road during the Han Dynasty and beyond, the cultural exchanges between China and the West before the Han Dynasty, dating back to 2000 B.C. or even earlier (the pre-Silk Road period), still have a long way to go. The perspective of observation should also be broader, paying due attention to the exchanges with the ancient Indus Valley.

Along with the in-depth study of the prehistory and Bronze Age archaeology of the Silk Road, the background of the Silk Road and the regional cultural interactions that existed at various times will be interpreted in a comprehensive and multi-dimensional manner, which will greatly contribute to the comprehension of the Silk Road and the cultural exchanges between China and the West.

In fact, the "Silk Road" is the inevitable result of thousands of years of cultural exchanges between East and West.

Beijing, China
November 2022

Dexin Cong

Contents

1. **Cultural Lineage Passed Down for Tens of Thousands of Years—Archaeological Excavations at the Site of Tongtian Cave in Jimunai County, Xinjiang** 1
   Jianjun Yu

2. **A Preliminary Analysis of Bronze Age Archaeological Culture in Xinjiang Region** 15
   Binghua Wang

3. **Relative Analogies in the Ritual Use of Red Mineral Pigments (Ochre, Hematite) in Neolithic and Eneolithic Burials from Xinjiang and Bulgaria** 31
   Maria Marinova

4. **An Archaeological Study of Early Nomadic Cultural Settlements in the Eastern Tianshan Mountain Region** 51
   Jianxin Wang and Lin Xi

5. **The 'Venetian' Silver Chalice of Feng Chao 馮朝 *Inventing Medieval Chinese Christianity in Fascist Italy*** 69
   Antonio De Caro

6. **A Comparative Study of Layouts of Buddhist Monasteries in Gandhāra Area and Tarim Basin** 87
   Xiao Li and Zhitang Liao

7. **PIXE Analysis of Glazed Ceramics of the Early Islamic Period at Hazara University Museum Collection** 111
   Shakirullah, Muhammad Zahoor, Ihsanullah Jan, and Abdul Basit

8. **Some Theoretical Issues in the Development of Prehistoric Civilizations in the Region of Xiyu** 123
   Tao Shui

Chapter 1
Cultural Lineage Passed Down for Tens of Thousands of Years—Archaeological Excavations at the Site of Tongtian Cave in Jimunai County, Xinjiang

Jianjun Yu

Abstract The Tongtian Cave site discovered in 2014 is located between the Altai Mountains and the Taerbahatai Mountains. It is not only the first Paleolithic site with clear stratigraphic relationships in Xinjiang at present, but also a comprehensive site encompassing the Chalcolithic Age, the Bronze Age, and the Early Iron Age. The work, which lasted for five years, made many important discoveries and opened the curtain on Paleolithic archaeology in Xinjiang and also made new discoveries about the history of Xinjiang around 10,000 years ago.

Keyword Tongtian Cave site · Integrated study · Paleolithic age · Wheat · Barley · Millet

From 2016 to 2020, the Xinjiang Institute of Cultural Relics and Archaeology, in cooperation with the School of Archaeology and Museum of Peking University, conducted five archaeological excavations at the Tongtian Cave site in Jimunai County, with a total excavation area of 241 m^2 and two excavation areas of caves and open fields. Cultural layer accumulations of the transition from the Middle to the Late Paleolithic period, more than 45,000 years ago, were unearthed, and more than 3000 pieces of various types of numbered specimens were unearthed, such as lithic, copper and bronze objects, iron tools, and animal fossils.

1.1 Geographical Location and Natural Environment

The site of Tongtian Cave is located in a granite cave in the northeast Kuoyitasi village, Tuosite town, Jimunai County, Altai Region, Xinjiang Uygur Autonomous Region. Jimnai County is located at the northern edge of the Junggar Basin, at the

---

J. Yu (✉)
Researcher of Institute of Cultural Relics and Archaeology in Xinjiang, Uygur Autonomous Region, Urumqi, China
e-mail: 279985611@qq.com

Fig. 1.1 Location of the site of Tongtian Cave (Photography by Yu Jianjun)

northern foot of the Sawuer Mountains, on the southern bank of the Eerqisi River, adjacent to Fuhai County in the east, connected to Bukesaier and the Tacheng region in the south, connected to Habahe and Buerjin counties in the north, and bordering with the Republic of Kazakhstan in the west, with a 141-km-long border (Fig. 1.1).

The area is classified as a moderate temperate continental climate zone, but the westerly circulation brings Atlantic water vapor, which drives down the valley of the Eerqisi River and the Tanzhaisan Valley in Kazakhstan and meets the Altai Mountains to the north forced to uplift and became precipitation, making the Altai region one of the abundant water areas in Xinjiang. The annual precipitation in the area where the site is located is above 300 mm, making the area not only excellent pasture for grazing now but also an important area suitable for the ancient human. A number of ancient remains from different periods have also been found around the Tongtian Cave site, such as the Jiangsaiti site, the Saerkuolacemetery, the Keziletuyuke cemetery, the Songshugou Kuolakesa stone tomb, the Sentasi cemetery, the Kuresala hilltop necropolis, and the Kezilekuola petroglyphs.

The site has three caves of different sizes, the frontal view is slightly "tripod mouth" shape, the left cave is the largest as the entrance is 22.5 m long, and the maximum depth is 27 m, and its height it 4.5 m. About 2 m into the cave, the cave merges with the peak of the mountain and it forms a shaft; thus, it is named Tongtian Cave. Because the cave was used as a livestock shed for a long time, there is a thick deposit of cattle and sheep's excrement on the surface of the cave, and so as the ashes. There are three small caves on the inner wall of the eastern part in cave, and the cave entrance on the north side was sealed with adobe, which may be related to

Fig. 1.2 Look of the site

the shed. There is also a small cave on the upper south side of the inner wall, which leads to the upper right side of the hillside. The smaller cave on the left side, which is almost filled with soil, has a deposit of about 30 m^2 at the entrance of the cave. According to the description of local herders, when it rains heavily, pottery pieces are often washed out from the deposit. Some remnants of stone mortar and pestle and hand-made sandy gray and red pottery sherds were also collected from this place. In addition to the plain surface of the pottery sherds, patterns on ceramic such as incised lines and folding lines made up of sticking lines were also visible. These pottery sherds and decorations are basically the same as those excavated from the tombs of the Qiemuerqieke culture (Fig. 1.2).

1.2 Work Overview

In 2014, during the first national census of movable cultural relics in Xinjiang, the Northern Xinjiang Cultural Relics Expert Group and the staff of the cultural relic bureau of the Altai region and Jimunai County found this site in Kuoyitasi village at Jimunai County and initially identified the site as a Bronze Age ancient human settlement site. In 2015, the Xinjiang Institute of Cultural Relics and Archaeology sent archaeological team to conduct a more detailed investigation of the site.

In early 2016, an excavation application was submitted to and approved by the National Administration of Cultural Heritage. In order to explore the scale and nature of the cave site, 5 × 5 quadrants were laid out inside Cave 1 and outside Cave 2 in order to excavate and recognize the archaeological cultural sequence and associated remains of the site. The surface of cattle and sheep excretion accumulation in cave 1 was thick, and after cleaning, the quadrant T1515 was set, and after cleaning the surface, archaeologists found the early Iron Age–Bronze Age cultural layers which were relatively thin, and a relatively pure yellow sand layer appeared in the southeast, which gradually expanded to the whole square. Then, excavators continued downward to clean up to the crushed rock deposit, under which many paleolithic artifacts and animal fossils were found. The Xinjiang Institute of Cultural Relics and Archaeology, in conjunction with the School of Archaeology and Museum of Peking University, conducted a trench of 4 m^2 of the area to initially determine the nature and age of the stone artifacts.

The excavation of quadrant T0505 which is at outside of Cave 2 exposed more pottery sherds and stone grinding plates as well as the remains of repetition of fire use and the probable remains of stone piles.

Based on this, the two archaeological institutes started to cooperate again to excavate the Tongtian Cave site four times in succession from 2017 to 2020. In addition to continuing the excavation of two small quadrants T0505 (total number T0118) and T1515, a small trench of 1 × 2 m, a small slate tomb, and seven other quadrants of 5 × 5 m^2 were excavated in the open area outside Tongtian Cave in order to understand the stratigraphy and the typology of remains, which exposed pits, hearth pit and pillar holes, and unearthed stone arrowheads, pottery sherds, copper tools, microlithic, and pottery spinning wheels. During the period, the Institute of Remote Sensing and Digital Earth Research of the Chinese Academy of Sciences was also invited to assist in the excavation area and the surrounding area of the site for electrical method and ground-penetrating radar exploration, which formed a preliminary inference to the site and the nearby stratigraphy.

At the same time, several archaeological surveys have been conducted in the surrounding area, and six lithic sites have been discovered and reviewed in the territory of Jimunai, Habahe, and Fuyun counties, and the collected stone artifacts have been sorted and studied.

1.3 Discoveries

Layers 6A ~ 9 of T1515 in Cave 1 are Paleolithic cultural deposit. A large number of stone artifacts, fossilized animal bones and ash mounds, and other remains were found.

Three ash deposit in situ were found in layers 8B ~ 9 of T1515.Two of them were superimposed together, and only its western side was unearthed, because the eastern side was located under the superimposed stratum unexcavated one ash pile with a clearer circular boundary. There are stone tools scattered on the surface of the ash deposit, and the sand close to the ash presents slightly redder than normal, so it probably related to the firing activity. In addition, black ashes of varying thickness, irregular shape, and unclear boundaries were found in most areas of layer 7, most likely as ash accumulations disturbed by flowing water (Fig. 1.3).

A total of 1259 numbered stone artifacts and 793 fossil animal specimens, totaling 2052 pieces, were excavated from the paleolithic strata of the Tongtian Cave site.

Fig. 1.3 T1515
(Photography by He Jianing)

In addition, more than 2000 pieces of smaller stone artifacts, including debris, and more than 9000 pieces of fossil animals, mainly small animals, with some of their identification characteristics, were also collected from screening. Most of the remains were excavated in layers 6B and 7, accounting for about 88% of all stone artifacts, but there was no significant change in the type and proportion of artifacts excavated in each layer.

The lithological variety of raw materials for stone products is diverse, with tuff, siliceous mudstone, and siliceous tuff predominating, and a certain proportion of andesite, quartz, and flint also present. Among them, siliceous tuff, siliceous mudstone, and flint account for more than one-third of the high-quality raw materials, which are mostly used for the production of delicate tools and larger size of Levallois products. The quality of raw materials such as amorphous tools, amorphous stone cores and simple stone flakes is relatively poor.

Overall, the stone artifacts from the Tongtian Cave site have typical Levallois factors, with typical Levallois flakes, Levallois cores, Levallois pointed tools, and Mousterian pointed tools together accounting for about 14.3% of the stone artifacts, and this percentage should be even higher given the considerable number of Levallois flakes used as rough artifacts. The choice of siliceous rock with better flaking properties is evident in this category, while simple flaked flakes, cores, and a large number of amorphous tools make more use of igneous rocks. Another notable feature of the Tongtian Cave lithic assemblage is the proportion of tools accounting for as much as 38.1% of the assemblage. Judged in conjunction with the small size of the cores, poor lithic material, and small number of broken pieces and debris found at the site, these tools should have been brought to the site after production was completed in areas other than produced in the cave (Fig. 1.4).

The Paleolithic strata of Tongtian Cave have identified animal species including rhinoceroses, brown bears, birds, carnivores, rabbits, sheep, donkeys, etc. The animal bones are highly fragmented, and some of them have obvious traces of cutting,

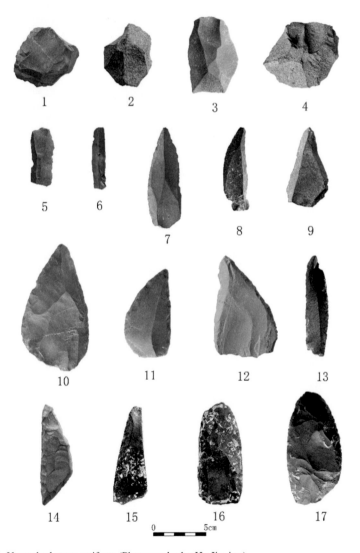

Fig. 1.4 Unearthed stone artifacts (Photography by He Jianing)

Fig. 1.5 T0505 ⑪(Photography by Chen Peng)

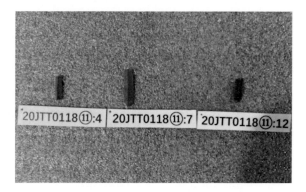

burning, and knocking. Burned bones account for a certain proportion of the animal bones. Combined with the phenomenon of ash deposit and other relics as well as the combination of stone products, these bones are obviously related to human activities. The sifted animal fragments are very small, with rodents, birds, and other small animals predominating.

A total of 11 stone artifacts were found in ② B layer T1515 in Cave 1, including complete stone flakes, broken flakes, broken blocks, etc., as well as one stone flake with a renewed platform and one fine microblade. All but one of the siltstone flakes use high-quality siliciclastic raw materials. The age of this layer is unknown, and because it is located below the Bronze Age stratigraphy, the possibility that its date may have entered the Holocene cannot be ruled out.

Three successive layers of T0505 (total number T0118), ⑩, ⑪, and ⑫layers outside Cave 2 were excavated with fine stone tools, which were dated by carbon 14, and concentrated in the period of 8900–13,000 years ago (Fig. 1.5).

The destroyed slate burials, pillar holes, pits, and hearth pits found outside Cave 2 T0505 as well as outside the cave in the flat area were found with more pottery sherds, stone tools, and a small amount of copper, iron, and bone tools. Among them, the pottery sherds have rim, bottom, and body, and most of them are the ceramic body part. As for the pattern, most of them are plain, and some of them have carved patterns on the surface. Stone tools include grinding plates, stone balls, etc. According to angle of the pottery rim, it can be inferred that there is wide flared mouth, converging mouth and other types. The decoration includes engraved pattern, embossed pattern, stamped pattern. The ear of the vessel has a raised ear, and the bottom of the vessel can be seen to be mostly flat-bottomed ware. Iron tool is iron knife, whereas the copper tools are arrowhead, copper cone. The bone tool is bone spoon (Figs. 1.6, 1.7, 1.8, 1.9, 1.10, 1.11, 1.12, 1.13, 1.14, 1.15 and 1.16).

Among the flotation plants, the main ones are millet, barley, and wheat, and we date the barley grains (Figs. 1.17, 1.18 and 1.19).

Fig. 1.6 T0505 ①:4 (Photography by Liu Yusheng)

Fig. 1.7 T0505 ④:1 (Photography by Liu Yusheng)

Fig. 1.8 T0505 ②:2 (Photography by Liu Yusheng)

1 Cultural Lineage Passed Down for Tens of Thousands … 9

Fig. 1.9 T0505 ④:5 (Pottery) (Photography by Liu Yusheng)

Fig. 1.10 T0505:6 (Photography by Liu Yusheng)

Fig. 1.11 T0505 ⑤:1 Pottery spinning reel (Photography by Liu Yusheng)

Fig. 1.12 T1515 ①:2 Iron knife (Photography by Liu Yusheng)

Fig. 1.13 T0505 ①:1 Iron cone (Photography by Liu Yusheng)

1.4 Summary

The Paleolithic cultural deposits were dated to about 45,000 years ago by 14C determination of faunal fossils.

The early Iron and Bronze Age stratigraphic deposits within T0505 were flotationally obtained from carbonized wheat (*Triticum aestivum* L.) and barley (*Hordeum vulgare* L.var. nudum Hook.f.), which were dated to 5200–3500 (Calibrated) years before present. This suggests that the Tongtian Cave site may be the earliest Chalcolithic Age site in Xinjiang.

1 Cultural Lineage Passed Down for Tens of Thousands … 11

Fig. 1.14 Copper cone (Photography by Deng Zhenhua)

Fig. 1.15 T0505 ④:2 (Photography by Deng Zhenhua)

Millet (Broomcorn millet) was found in the same stratum as wheat barley, and it is dated at about 4400 years ago. Further work and research on this need to be done in depth.

The Tongtian Cave site is a comprehensive cave site, the first Paleolithic site in Xinjiang that has been excavated and found to have clear stratigraphy. Five years of excavation have shown that the site has a long-term occupation, with the deepest part of the excavation area being about 3 m from the surface, and a continuous

Fig. 1.16 T0505 ②:6 (Photography by Deng Zhenhua)

Fig. 1.17 Millet carbide

Fig. 1.18 Barley carbide

1 Cultural Lineage Passed Down for Tens of Thousands … 13

Fig. 1.19 Wheat carbide

stratigraphic profile of Paleolithic–Chalcolithic (possibly Neolithic)–Bronze–Early Iron age was found. The clear sequence of accumulations and the large chronological span of the site not only fill the gap of prehistoric Paleolithic archaeology in Xinjiang but also represent a major discovery of Paleolithic archaeology in China, which is very important for understanding the evolutionary development of ancient humans in the Xinjiang region since more than 40,000 years and establishing a chronological framework of regional cultural development.

The Tongtian Cave site is the first site that has clear and continuous stratigraphy buried with fine microlithic in Xinjiang dating from 8900 to 13,000 years ago; it is also the earliest Bronze Age site in Xinjiang at present.

The remains found in the Early Iron and Bronze Age strata include pottery, bronze, iron, and stone grinding plates, etc. The pottery sherds show that the Eurasian steppe Bronze Age resembles the Afanashevo and Qiemuerqieke cultures and the Early Iron Age culture of the Altai region.

The stone artifacts excavated from the Paleolithic culture layer are very rich, including Levallois stone cores, disk-shaped stone cores, Levallois pointed tools, various types of scrapers and Mousterian pointed tools, and other typical stone artifacts of the Levallois-Mousterian culture. The overall shows more obvious Middle Paleolithic cultural characteristics of the western side of the Old World, which is very unique among domestic sites of the same period and fills the gap of the typical Middle Paleolithic Mousterian culture type in China. Animal bones are highly fragmented, with obvious traces of cutting, burning, and striking, and identifiable species include carnivorous, rabbits, sheep, donkeys, rhinoceroses, brown bears, and a large number of small animal bones such as birds, which provide valuable information for exploring the way humans used animal resources and the environmental changes of the site during this period.

The typical Mousterian cultural remains excavated from the site are only found in a few sites in China, mainly in the northwest and northern regions of China, while such remains have been studied and found in Siberia, Mongolia, and other places in

Russia around China. The special geographical location and the typical Mousterian cultural remains excavated in the Altai region of Xinjiang, where the Tongtian Cave site is located, provide important clues to further explore the migration, exchange, and dispersal of people in the prehistoric period of Pleistocene Asia and Europe. It has great research potential and academic value in exploring ancient human adaptation methods, subsistence behavior, stone sources, paleo environmental studies, and chronology.

The earliest wheat and barley in China were found in the site, and the earliest millet in Xinjiang was also found, and it accounted for more than 60% of the crops discovered. This is something that should be of concern. After the millet crop was domesticated in North China about 9000 years ago, it began to spread in all directions, spreading to Tongtian Cave in the last 5000 years, so it can be assumed that there was a channel for the exchange of millet and wheat in Tongtian Cave 5000 years ago, which is of great significance for the study of the spread of early crops and their related cultures.

Archaeological investigations in recent years have revealed that the Tongtian Cave site is a comprehensive relic with extremely rich cultural deposit. As the entrance of Cave 1 and Cave 2 faces west, there is a strong west wind in winter, so the cave is not suitable for human survival, and they should live under the huge leeward sunrise rock wall opposite in winter. Behind the rock wall is a relatively closed, north-facing "U"-shaped quadrangle surrounded by natural rock, also suitable for human habitation. When we got across the road under the rock, we also found a cave; on the core area around the site, there are nine ancient cemeteries from the Bronze Age to the early Iron Age and a small site, nearly 1 km northwest of the discovery of a large rock shed.

Overall, the Tongtian Cave site is not only an important discovery of Paleolithic archaeology, but also a major breakthrough in the construction of a prehistoric archaeological and cultural sequence in northern Xinjiang. The relatively flat valley between the Altai Mountains and the Taerbahatai Mountains has been an important cultural transmission and exchange channel since the Paleolithic, and this feature is also expressed in the remains of the Bronze Age and the Early Iron Age, which has laid a consistent groundwork for the prehistoric archaeology of the Altai region. On January 8, 2018, the site of Tongtian Cave in Jimunai County was selected for the Chinese Academy of Social Sciences Archaeology Forum-2017 New Discoveries in Chinese Archaeology (Six Major Discoveries). On April 16, it was selected for the "2017 National Top Ten New Archaeological Discoveries."

Chapter 2
A Preliminary Analysis of Bronze Age Archaeological Culture in Xinjiang Region

Binghua Wang

Abstract This paper represents a kind of reflection and discussion in the archaeological community at the beginning of the discovery of Bronze Age remains in Xinjiang in the 1980s, which initially outlined the distribution and cultural landscape of Bronze Age remains in Xinjiang, and was very forward looking and inspiring at the time. Of course, as archaeological discoveries and research continue to evolve, the understanding of Bronze Age archaeological culture in Xinjiang is constantly being updated and developed on the basis of these early studies.

Keywords Bronze age · Xinjiang archaeology · Archaeological culture

The Bronze Age archaeological culture in Xinjiang is still a new proposition to be studied, both in terms of its absolute date and specific cultural connotations, and there is no article yet published to analyze and explore this aspect. In other words, this is still a gap to be filled in the field of archaeology in Xinjiang.

The important monographs published in China on bronzes, such as Rong Geng's "General Examination of Yi Vessels of the Shang and Zhou Dynasties" and Guo Baojun's "Chinese Bronze Age", came out earlier, and the information was mostly about the bronze culture of the Central Plains without a word about that of Xinjiang. The recent tome "Important Archaeological Discoveries and Research in New China", published for the 35th anniversary of the founding of New China, still does not say a word about the Bronze Age archaeological culture in Xinjiang, even though it accounts for one-sixth of the country's area. This reflects the weakness of research in this area. This problem is not, of course, due to any special circumstances of the archaeological culture of Xinjiang, which has transcended the Bronze Age stage of development. On the contrary, since liberation, many significant sites and tombs of this period have been found in Xinjiang, and many important bronze artifacts have been unearthed in industrial and agricultural production. The main leading factors for

---

B. Wang (✉)
Researcher of Institute of Cultural Relics and Archaeology in Xinjiang, Uygur Autonomous Region, Urumqi, China
e-mail: wbh35@126.com

this situation are that archaeologists in Xinjiang are not sufficiently aware of some major discoveries in this area to report them in time and that the reported discoveries have not been analyzed thoroughly with necessary generalizations and studies. These obvious weaknesses naturally limit the understanding of the problem and affect the depth of the research. On the basis of the present work, it is very difficult to make a clearer and more accurate description of the main aspects of the Bronze Age archaeological culture in Xinjiang. However, a preliminary overview of the existing data and an analysis applying certain **theories** will obviously promote the depth of the problem. Therefore, what I have proposed here is only a preliminary view of the beginning and peak of the Bronze Age in Xinjiang, its basic characteristics and its relationship with surrounding areas. To some extent, it can only be said to be an opinion for discussion. We hope that in further discussions, especially in the future practice, we will be able to revise it and gradually improve it.

According to the available archaeological data, my personal opinion is that from the second millennium B.C., Xinjiang had started coming into the Bronze Age. Around the first millennium B.C., the bronze culture was quite prosperous and the use of bronze tools was quite common. Copper mining also became mature. In the late Warring States period, iron tools appeared and the transformation to the Iron Age was gradually realized. Due to the geographical location of Xinjiang, the bronze vessels are closely related to the neighboring Central Asian region in terms of shape and style. It also shared the distinctive regional characteristics with wares from the Mongolian steppe, with.

I

Two reasons led tomy proposal that during the second millennium B.C., Xinjiang had already entered the Bronze Age: One is the excavation of the Gumugou cemetery in the Lop Nur area, and the other is a bronze artifact collected in Ageersen, Gongliu County, in the Yili River valley. Although we currently only have two points, they involve a fairly large area.

In the winter of 1979, the Xinjiang Institute of Archaeology sent people to the Lop Nur area to conduct an archaeological survey, and on the basis of that, in the lower reaches of the Kongqi River, archaeologists started the excavation of Gumugou cemetery. I presided over this work. Other participants include Yidiliesi Abdu, Xing Kaiding, Liu Yusheng and Hou Can, Chang Xi'en, etc. Forty-two ancient tombs were unearthed. Burial can be distinguished into two main types. The first type is shaft tomb with wooden coffin, but it is shallow burial, and most of the time the wooden burial equipment is well preserved. The second type is also shaft tomb, but it was buried deep with decayed burial equipment. Outside the tomb, there are seven rings of wood, and outside that, stakes were put in four directions radically. One well-preserved tomb was observed to equip with total of 894 stakes. From the analysis of the burial form and excavated artifacts, the second type of burial is relatively late. Regarding the absolute date, according to several groups of data, the remains of the first type are dated to 3800 years ago. In both types of burials in this cemetery, small bronze coils and pieces were found. These small objects coexist with wood, stone (fine stone arrows), bone, jade ornaments, wheat seeds, straw products, woolen fabrics (cloth, blankets, felts) and livestock hides. The small bronze pieces are not only too tiny to identify their form, but also seriously decayed. It is difficult to determine the technique of bronze production or to analyze the role of bronze objects in social production at that time. So, it did not attract sufficient attention at that time.[1]

After a careful observation and analysis of the wooden tools and stakes excavated, we started to pay more attention to them. A detailed analysis of the traces preserved on related artifacts is discovered in the cemetery, and we have to draw the conclusion that in the Gumugou area at that time, the use of a type of rather sharp metal cutting tools is of no doubt. Because they are too hard and sharp for grinding stone or red copper tools to shape into, the most reasonable tool would be a bronze one. Therefore, although no large bronze tools have been excavated from this cemetery, it also provides convincing evidence for our understanding of the Bronze Age culture in Xinjiang.

Because of the very dry environment, most of the wood, bone, fur and other artifacts in the cemetery are as intact as they were when buried. The nondecaying wooden boards still sound when knocked at. Upon those planks, a large number of traces left by processing tools are clearly discernible. To determine the nature of the tools and their sharpness, a study of the traces would contribute a lot.

The wood used in the cemetery is mostly diversifolius populus. It is fine and hard. It is not easy to cut and flatten the trunks of the populus, whose diameter is 20–30 cm long, for producing coffins or stakes. Forty-two tombs were excavated in the Gumugou cemetery, the first type of burial accounting for thirty-six. There are wooden "coffins" almost in all burials. After placing compartment boards and stall boards into a sand cave, the corpse was put into the "coffin", with a number of small wooden boards upon it to seal it. These boards, made of populus, were cut into relatively flat plates with a relatively consistent length and thickness and neat edges. It is obviously the result of a handy tool. Although the second type of burial tools is decaying, there are many well-preserved wooden stakes and pillars. One end of the thick populus wood with a diameter of 20–30 cm had to be sharpened into a sharp point in order to be inserted deep into the ground. I have observed and recorded the situation of a thick wood with a diameter of 23 cm and a length of 110 cm, one of whose ends was cut into a very sharp pointed cone. The cone was 28 cm long and its sharp end is less than a centimeter, the cut marks both polished and neat. We collected and studied the statistics of the clearly cut-marked burial tools and stakes that were taken back to Urumqi. From the two hundred and forty pieces of data, it can be seen that the chopping marks are caused by cutting tools. The width of the blade is generally from three to five centimeters, the narrowest 1.5 cm. The marks

---

[1] I have briefly introduced the information in the article "Excavation and Preliminary Study of the Gumugou in Kongque River" (in Xinjiang Social Science, 1983, 1) and suggested that this is a cultural relic of the Neolithic period. According to the analysis of the Xinjiang Metallurgical Research Institute, the small bronze pieces found in the cemetery are believed to be red copper. The specimens were sent to the Institute of Metallurgical History of Beijing Iron and Steel Institute for further analysis. In particular, according to the large number of metal tool marks preserved in the cemetery relics, it indicates that metal tools were commonly used. The owner of the cemetery must have entered the Bronze Age.

are quite smooth and clean. The first cut was as deep as 10.5 cm, and the general depth was three to five centimeters. The depth, smoothness and cleanliness of the cut show that they cannot be achieved by any blunt, light non-metal tool. In other words, only the sharper, heavier metal axes can make such a cut. In the cemetery, many wooden figures, cups and plates were also discovered. Some of the wooden tools were hollowed out in accordance with its original shape, which is not exquisite. But there is no shortage of finely processed specimens. For example, a carefully carved wooden female figurine featured the character's pointed felt hat, braid, pointed chin and plump but dropping breasts. The carving of the braid is neat and clear beside the forehead. The hat, chin and breasts are all very evenly carved with clean and sharp cutting marks.

I had the opportunity to observe the experiment of using a stone axe to cut and process wooden articles. A large, sharp-edged stone axe was used to cut a small tree, and in ten minutes or so, the tree with a diameter of 10 cm could be cut off. Some traces were left behind: The cut marks are very rough; the finished surface is coarse and uneven; each time, the depth of cutting is barely or less than one centimeter. This is quite different from the cutting marks on the wooden piles, coffins and woodwork of the ancient tomb ditch cemetery, no matter in terms of the depth or the smoothness of the cut. Such a deep and clean-cut obviously requires a sharp blade and a quite heavy axe.

It should also be noted that if such cutting marks exist only in a few cases, other possibilities can be considered. However, the conclusion of the present observation is that in any burial, any piece of wooden artifact, coffin, column of wooden stakes and a large number of cutting marks with the same characteristic scan be found. Thus, this is a universal phenomenon. The specimens of funerary objects and stakes we retrieved from Urumqi for analysis offer a very small and disproportionate amount of information compared to the wood unearthed from the cemetery. These specimens were randomly selected and observed. Among them, there are 240 sets of wood with similar cutting marks. This is sufficient to show that in the Gumugou area at that time, metal production tools had played an important role in social production and were not for occasional use. Common sense tells us that because red copper is soft and not hard enough, it could not exclude or replace stone tools in production. The sharp cut marks seen in the cemetery of Gumugou, which are four or five centimeters long in general, the deepest more than ten centimeters, are beyond the reach of red bronze and stone tools. Only bronze tools, or harder and sharper tools than bronze, can produce such an effect. From the analysis of the whole historical background, bronze is the most appropriate material for this kind of metal tools. Therefore, although we have not seen any bronze tools actually, it is reasonable to conclude that bronze tools were mainly used at that time. If this is the case, why is not a single bronze tool found in the whole cemetery? The main reason for this may be that these metal tools were a very valuable means of production at that time, and it was not easy to obtain them. Moreover, these tools were not generally used for burial because of their great relevance to people's real economic interests.

Since the logical deduction shows that during the construction period of Gumugou, there had been quite sharp bronze tools which can be used for cutting hardwood and processing boards especially in social production. Thus, it is natural to conclude that such a historical stage is part of the Bronze Age. Of course, this conclusion has yet to be proved by further discovery of material evidence. But we can believe that it is only a matter of time.

Similar in age to the Gumugou cemetery, another group of bronze tools were found in Gongli County in the Yili River valley of Northern Xinjiang. In 1975, Wang Bo and Cheng Zhenguo of Xinjiang Museum collected 12 bronze tools in Gongliu. They were unearthed in Ageersen (阿格尔森). The people dug a water channel here and found three axes, three sickles, three zheng (a kind of musical instrument) and three chisels at a depth of more than one meter from the surface, all bronze and making a total of twelve pieces.[2] With two sizes, the axes have arc blades curved handles decorated with leaf patterns and round holes to hold the handle. The sickles have curved back and edge, with obvious signs of use and heavy wear. The twelve bronze tools are all practical production tools and a large proportion of agricultural production tools. After the bronze tools were unearthed, their metal composition was analyzed by the Institute of Metallurgical History of the Beijing Steel Institute, which concluded that they were undoubtedly bronze tools.

Due to the unofficial excavation, it is not possible to provide more specific information about the archaeological culture of this collection of bronze materials. However, the form of the bronze axes and sickles is basically the same as that of those excavated from the Andronovo culture in the neighboring Soviet Union, and the decoration of the leaf pattern is identical. There is no doubt that this provides a strong clue to the absolute date of the bronzes in question. The so-called Andronovo culture is an archaeological culture of Kazakhstan, South Altai and Siberia in Russia, and its absolute date is between the fourth and third millennium. So, the absolute date of the bronze tools in our country should also be within such a historical stage, which is similar to that of the Gumugou cemetery.

In this way, the two batches of materials provide us with a very important explanation: from the Lop Nur region to the Yili River valley, in this very wide area, since the fourth millennium, people have used bronze. Of course, these two examples are not enough to fully explain the depth and breadth of the use of bronze in Xinjiang at that time; but as an indication of the use of bronze in Xinjiang, they are of no doubt.

II

Large bronze artifacts, which were around 3000 BP, were found in many locations in Xinjiang. A few sites and tombs where bronze artifacts were found have been excavated, and a certain amount of excavated material has been obtained. This is a strong indication that the bronze culture in Xinjiang had developed significantly during this period of history. Settlement and a considerable degree of agricultural development were important features of economic life in this period. In some areas, such bronze culture sites may prove that there has been a class society.

---

[2] Information about the Ageersen bronze tool. Provided by Comrade Cheng Zhenguo, who worked with Wang Bo. The bronze tools are now displayed in the Xinjiang Museum's "Xinjiang Historical Relics".

A few examples are given for illustration below.

At the southern foothill of Tianshan Mountain, in Xintala, Heshuo County, an ancient settlement site was discovered and excavated.[3] The lime soil in the cultural layer of the site is more than five meters thick, indicating that ancient people had a stable residence here for a long time. Copper, stone axes, jade axes, large stone knives, stone sickles, grain grinders, a large amount of painted and incised pottery, wheat and millet seeds and broken animal bones have been found in the site. Among the pottery, a large proportion of polychrome pottery was found. Before the archaeologists investigated and excavated the site, it had already suffered considerable damage during the process of fertilizing their fields by farmers. During this process, bronze axes, bronze knives and small bronze ornaments were found. Of particular note is a bronze axe-like object (No. 79HSx: 8), whose height is 17.3 cm. The blade is curved and hollowed out. The handle is perpendicular to the blade. The socket part is 3 cm wide, and the depth is 8 cm. Wide and curved, the blade has been used and is heavily damaged. The handle part has three ridges, which are slightly mutilated. The lower two ridges have been linked into a circle, which can be pendant accessories. The shape of the object is similar to that of an axe, but there are some features that are clearly different from those of an axe. The residual weight is 997 g, which shows that the original vessel must have weighed more than one kilogram. This is a practical production tool or weapon. The absolute date of this site according to the charcoals excavated from the cultural layer which were sent to the Carbon 14 laboratory of Bureau of Cultural Heritage Institute was 3640 ± 145 years ago.[4]

A Bronze Age settlement site has been excavated in Lanzhouwanzi in Balikun County in recent years. At the northern foot of Tianshan Mountain, especially in the territory of Balikun County, such as the sites of salt pond in the east Koumenzi, the military horse farm of Yiwu in the west Koumenzi, Kuisu, Shirenzi, Lanzhouwanzi, in the front of Tianshan Mountain, you can see a lot of giant mounds of earth and stone. The villagers commonly call these mounds of earth and stone "green pimples", "gray pimples", "white pimples", "black pimples", etc. At Shirenzi, Kui Su and other places, because of the villagers' digging for fertilizer, in this kind of giant mounds of earth and stone, there have been unearthed large grain grinder, polychrome pottery, small wheat grain, copper, etc. The excavation of cultural relics in the Shirenzi area has been reported.[5] About the unearthed artifacts of the Kuisu site, there is a story. In 1978, I worked in Balikun. When the villagers found a number of cultural relics,

---

[3] The artifacts found at Xintala site in Heshuo County are earlier. I had conducted a survey in 1979 and collected grinding stone tools, polychrome pottery and small pieces of copper blocks, in 1981. In 1981, the Xinjiang Institute of Archaeology and the Museum of Cultural Relics sent teams to conduct test excavations here. The excavated artifacts are now in the Xinjiang Archaeological Institute. One of the excavators, Lv Enguo, has already completed the report, which will be published soon.

[4] The measurement data are now in the Xinjiang Archaeological Institute and have not yet been published.

[5] Wu Zhen: "Several Neolithic sites in eastern Xinjiang", Archaeology, 1964, 7, and in the section on the Shirenzixiang site in Balikun County; Li Yichun, "The polychrome ceramic found in Xinjiang", Archaeology, 1959, 3. In these two articles, about the site of Shirenzixiang site, it is considered to be the cultural remains of the chalcolithic period. According to the excavation in Lanzhouwanzi

I immediately went to the scene to observe and recollected several pieces of bronze and pottery. The artifacts are now stored in the Balikun County Museum of Culture. Among the artifacts unearthed from Kuisu site, in addition to a large number of large grinding stones, polychrome pottery and red pottery pieces, there are also a large number of burnt ash and several bronze wares, including bronze axe, knife, sickle, etc. The axe is 21 cm long and 4–4.6 cm wide. It is oriented in the same direction as the axe blade by the handle. The diameter of the handle is 3.7 cm and is heavily eroded in green. The shape of the axe is characterized by three ridges from the end of the handle, extending toward the blade, which is marked with slashes. The small bronze knife is broken. The length of the broken blade is 8.5 cm, and its width is 2.8 cm. The handle has a nearly triangular ring hole, and the whole body is green. The bronze Dun is 11 cm in height. The handle part is a circle hole with a diameter of 2.2 cm. The part for inserting into ground is flat and cone shaped, but there are no signs of use. Besides, there are also ceramic and stone containers unearthed. Regarding the absolute date of the Kuisu site, carbon 14 dating was conducted on the charcoals taken from the mound, and the conclusion was 2620 ± 70 years ago.[6]

In recent years, the Institute of Archaeology of Xinjiang Academy of Social Sciences has excavated a giant stone mound site in Lanzhouwanzi which is about six kilometers west to Balikun County. The stone mound on the surface is circular shaped, with a diameter of 30 m and a height of 3 m. The surface features are consistent with the stone mounds seen in Shirenzi and Kuisu. The excavation results show that this type of mound is actually a building made of huge stones. It was abandoned and covered with earth. The area of the building is nearly 200 m², surrounded by stone walls, with a thickness of 3 m and a height of nearly 2 m. It is divided into front and back rooms. The main room is in the south, with an area of 100 m². There are pillar holes, the remnants of wooden pillars still remaining in them. The main room and the back room are connected to each other by a doorway. The door is opened to the east from the annex room. The material used for the stone wall was selected from the giant stone in front of the mountain, and the large one was 1.5 m in length, 50–60 cm in width and thickness and was too heavy to be moved by one person. However, the inner wall of the house is very flat. In the house, a large amount of charcoal and burned red ash was found. At the same time, excavators unearthed a large ring-footed bronze Fu, a small ring-headed bronze knife, a double-eared drum-belly red pottery jar, a polychrome pottery jar, a pottery polisher, a number of large grinding stones and stone balls, carbonized small wheat grains and horse, sheep and deer bones. The bronze Fu is 54 cm in height and 32 cm in diameter. It has a flat mouth and double-ears. Its belly was decorated with a wave pattern, and the bottom is a ring foot. The surface is green with some parts covered smoky black. All the potteries are handmade. The stone site has been inhabited three times at least. Excavators took the charcoal from the bottom layer and sent it to the Institute of Cultural Preservation for

---

and the collection in Kuisu, large bronze artifacts were found in these sites. It is believed to be the cultural remains of the Bronze Age.

[6] "Carbon 14 dating dataset in Chinese archaeology", Wenwu Press, p. 152.

carbon 14 dating, and the conclusion is 3285 ± 75 years ago, indicating the earliest time of the site.[7]

It is noteworthy that the same shape of the bronze Fu discovered at Lanzhouwanzi ancient settlement site was also found at other places, such as in Balikun Dahe Commune, Qitai County Karz Town, West Karz group and other places. The bronze Fu unearthed at West Karz is 40 cm high and together with scratching gray pottery. Such a large area and a long period of time indicate that the archaeological culture represented by Lanzhouwanzi, which unearthed a large bronze Fu, is a group of cultural sites worthy of attention.

The excavated materials from Kermuqi are also in the cultural stage of the Bronze Age. At the southern foot of the Altai Mountains, the excavations at Kermuqi, Altai County, of stone figures and sarcophagi and shaft tombs have a complex cultural content and a rather long history. The original brief had correctly revealed this substance. However, that the earliest date of the materials is the Warring States period is a conclusion that can be further discussed.[8] I have participated in the excavation of Kermuqi and have personally excavated a considerable part of all the 32 burials. Therefore, I am more familiar with the situation of the burials. Here the sarcophagus tombs have relatively obvious early characteristics. Their basic characters are there are stone figurines in front of the sarcophagus and other coffins. Most of the coffins hold a cluster of dead bodies, some even with the skeletons of up to 20 people. Burial artifacts are stone and bronze arrowheads, bronze knives, stone cups, jars and gray pottery (multi-ring bottom, olive-like shape, decorated with scratches) and so on.

The pottery shape and decoration are clearly related to the neighboring Russia's Avanashevo culture.[9] It is also believed that the "stone vessels and olive-shaped pottery excavated here are the typical objects of this basic burial area. They are quite similar to the artifacts of the Karasuk culture in the South Altai region of Russia and are believed to date from around 1200–700 B.C.E.[10] However, there is no specific explanation for this view. It is true that the pottery from the Karasuk culture in the Soviet Union also includes a duck-egg-shaped jar with a cedar needle pattern, which Russian scholars also consider to have "preserved the tradition of the Avanashevo".[11] From this point of view, it is possible to agree with each other. However, according to this, the absolute date of such burials in Kermuqi is much earlier than the Han Dynasty or the Warring States period, which can be clearly affirmed. In this case, the Bronze Age stage in the Altay area must have been before one thousand B.C.

In the same era, a group of Ordos-style bronzes were unearthed in Chaqimale of Garden Commune in the southern suburbs of Hami. The bronze tools were buried

---

[7] The excavation data and chronological conclusions are available at the Xinjiang Institute of Archaeology. The general situation of the excavations and the main excavated artifacts were reported in Xinjiang Daily 1985, 5. The Xinjiang Yearbook 1984 also reported on the excavations.

[8] Briefing on the Excavation of the Ancient Tomb Group in Kermuzi, Xinjiang, Cultural Relics 1, 1981, p. 27–32.

[9] Gishelev, "Ancient History of South Siberia", Chapter 2.

[10] Mu Shunying and Wang Mingzhe, "Ancient Ethnic Archaeological Culture in Xinjiang", Xinjiang Social Science Research, No. 6, 1985.

[11] Gishelev, "Ancient History of South Siberia", Chapter 2.

four meters below the surface and were excavated by the community members. A deer-headed bronze knife was found. (The overall length of the handle is 13.5 cm. The end of the handle is a circular carved deer head. The deer has a long face, a pair of bulging eyes, erect ears and antlers which form a ring. The head of the handle and the back of the knife are curved into a harmonious arc) There was also a small bronze knife with a ring as its end. (Its overall length is 14.5 cm, and the handle length is 6.5 cm. The handle is slightly curved, with a triangular ring at the end of the handle. The knife has a curved back and a slightly convex blade). Moreover, there is a bronze arrowhead (leaf-shaped with a socket, overall length 5.8 cm) and sharpening stone. The excavated pottery was destroyed by the villagers. This group of bronze artifacts has the typical Ordos style. Bronze knives of the same shape have been found in the Ordos region of Inner Mongolia, Qinglong County, Hebei Province and the Shang Dynasty site of Yantou village in Suide, Shaanxi Province, and also in the neighboring Russia's Karasok culture. According to the excavation information of Qinglong County, the popular era of similar deer-headed bronze knives is from the late Shang Dynasty to the early Western Zhou Dynasty.[12]

In the Hami area, there are some other sites where bronze tools around this period were also excavated, like the ancient cemetery of Wubao Commune in Hami County. More than 30 burials were excavated, the artifacts include the fur and woolen fabrics of the deceased, wooden, stone, pottery (including polychrome pottery) and sea shells. The deceased have small bronze ornaments on clothes and shoes, and the male deceased wears sharpening stones and small bronze knives at the waist. The bronze knives are green in color and have a one-sided blade. Because of the dry climate of the Wubao cemetery, the fabrics and woodwork are mostly well preserved. The wood on the tomb is also well preserved. From the tool marks left on the unearthed wood, we can see that the cut marks on the rather hard populus wood are quite polished and the cuts are very sharp. The size and length of the cover wood are consistent, and the shape is regular. By the same token, a hard, sharp bronze metal tool is the only reason to leave such a trace. The absolute date of this cemetery was determined by carbon dating using the tomb's cover wood, which was concluded to be between 1165 and 890 B.C.[13]

A cemetery of the same age as the Wubao cemetery was also found at Sibao Lafuqiaoke in Hami. A distinctive feature is the coexistence of polychrome pottery and bronze.[14]

In 1975, an ancient site was also excavated in Turpan County. At a depth of more than one meter from the surface, polychrome pottery, red-brown pottery and bronze arrowhead were found at the site Halahezhuo. On the surface of the site, a tiger-shaped bronze plaque was collected. The excavation of this site was not finalized.

---

[12] Hami excavated cultural relics, now collected in Hami City Museum of Culture. I have conducted a survey in the excavated area. The relevant information will be published soon.

[13] The artifacts excavated from Wubao, Hami, are now in the Xinjiang Archaeological Institute. For a brief description, see "Thirty Years of Archaeology in Xinjiang", p. 3. Xinjiang People's Publishing House, 1983. For the dating, see Carbon 14 Dating in Chinese Archaeology, p. 152, Xinjiang Publishing House, 1983.

[14] "Late Neolithic burial found in Lafuqike, Xinjiang", Archaeology and Cultural Relics, 1984, 4.

Charcoal was taken from the cultural layer of the site for dating, and it was concluded that the site was 2895 ± 100 years ago.[15]

The cultural relics team of Xinjiang Museum has excavated more than a hundred ancient burials at the Nanwan Cemetery of Kuisu Commune, Balikun County. Among the unearthed artifacts, there is a number of copper axes, small copper knives, polychrome pottery, red and brown pottery and stone tools. The shape of the bronze knife is the same as that excavated in Hami Wubao site. The general characteristics seem to be similar to those of Balikun, Kuisu, Shirenzi and Hami Wubao cemeteries.[16]

Other sites, such as the Sidaogou site in Mulei County, have also been discovered with bronze vessels in the early cultural layer 3000 years ago. These small bronze objects coexist with polished stone tools, bone tools and pottery.[17] The late cultural layer of the Kaersang site in Yiwu County yielded stone jars and bronze objects.[18] At the ancient site of Kalayuergun in Akesu County, bronze rings were found underground at a depth of four meters from the surface.[19] In addition to these sites, other sites, such as the upper reaches of the Gongnaisi River, the Chabuha River site and the Tielishigai site in Tekesi County, have also collected bronze knives, bronze axes and bull's head-shaped bronze ornaments.

As we have listed these ancient sites, we can see that their distribution was quite extensive. A conclusion is that the use of bronze tools was common in Xinjiang around 3000 years ago.

III

More Bronze Age sites dating back from the middle of the first millennium B.C. to the Warring States period were found throughout Xinjiang. Many sites of the Warring States period have been discovered with iron tools such as small iron knife, iron arrowhead, iron nails and so on. This phenomenon suggests that in the Warring States period, Xinjiang region has begun to move toward the Iron Age.

In order to further understand the archaeological culture of the Bronze Age in Xinjiang, the copper mining and smelting production in this period is an important part that should be paid attention to. Xinjiang is not rich from the point of view of copper and tin deposits. However, there are many copper ore sites. Many sites have been exploited in the past, such as Tekesi County's Jingbulake, Nileke County's Nulasai Mountain, Urumqi region's Dabancheng and Hami region's Shaquanzi. At the periphery of Tarim Basin, there are Aketao County's Kalama, Tegelisuman, Baicheng County Dishui, Aerbalieke in Shache County, Kekenaike in Tuokexun County, etc. In Nileke County, Nulasai, Quantoushan, Baicheng County's Dishui,

---

[15] Carbon 14 Dating Data in Chinese Archaeology, Cultural Heritage Press, 1983.

[16] Nanwan excavation data, stored in the Xinjiang Museum, have not been published. However, some of the artifacts have been exhibited in the display of historical artifacts in Xinjiang Museum and the display of artifacts in Balikun County, so we can see its overview.

[17] Xinjiang Cultural Management Committee, "Excavations at the Sidaogou Site in Mulei County", Archaeology, 1982, 2.

[18] Wu Zhen, "Several Neolithic sites in eastern Xinjiang", Archaeology, 1964, 7.

[19] "The Ancient Sites of Kalayuergun in Akesu", in Thirty Years of Archaeology in Xinjiang, Xinjiang People's Publishing House, 1983, pp. 38–39.

we also found ancient mining traces. These copper deposits are not very large, and they are buried shallow which are easy to mine. Besides, the copper content is rich. As for tin, in the Botala area of the upper reaches of the right tributary of the Tuergong River Valley, there is a considerable number of deposits.[20] Undoubtedly, these copper and tin deposits are a favorable material basis for the development of the bronze manufacturing industry in the Xinjiang region.

Among these copper sites, mining and smelting sites from the Spring and Autumn Period and the Warring States period have been found in Yuntoushan and Nulasai Mountain in Nileke County.

The ancient copper mine sites of Yuantou Mountain and Nulasai Mountain are located in the low hilly area on the north slope of Ajinlale Mountain and the south bank of Kashi River in Nileke County. The ancient pit of Yuantou Mountain is about five kilometers away from the county. It is called Yuantou (roundhead) Mountain because the shape of the mountain resembles an isolated bell-shaped hill. At the top of the mountain, there are two fractured zones along 320°NW, filled with copper-bearing quartz-calcite, partly covered by sand, but with pot-shaped depressions, which can be traced to the mine. The results of trenching along the ore passage show a large accumulation of waste ore below one meter of sand cover, and there is no bedrock below two meters.

The pot-shaped depressions along the passage are remnants of ancient mining pits. The opening of the pit is 2.5 m in diameter, the bottom 1 m in diameter and the depth 2 m. It is covered with sand soil and bushes. From the analysis of the spreading situation: mining at that time was at intervals to seek ore rich in copper, and the deepest depth has been mined to three meters below.

Along the ore passage of Yuantou Mountain, a large number of waste ore piles were found under the sand clay complex. In the waste ore pile, there are many flat round, almond-shaped, ovoid stone tools more than 10–20 cm in diameter, and the waist of the stones has groove marks which are about two centimeters wide in a rounded edge. Some of them have break-off gap, obviously it is the traces of use. The stones are mostly granite, quartz sodic porphyry, siliceous siltstone, etc. The stone is taken from the riverbed of Kashi River and the nearby diorite conglomerate. Together with the lithics, there are fragments of wood carbon. These carbon blocks were dated by the laboratory of the Department of Archaeology of Peking University, and the date was 2650 ± 170 years ago, which corresponds to the Spring and Autumn Period.

At the copper mine site of Yuantou Mountain, only such open pit mining and large stone tools were discovered. Although wood charcoal was also found, there is no trace of further smelting.[21]

---

[20] The relevant information, except for the archaeological survey conducted by archaeologists in Nulasai Mountain, Nileke County, is based on the information provided by Comrade Wu Shaozu, an engineer at the Scientific Research Institute of Xinjiang Geological Bureau, for which we hereby express our gratitude.

[21] Yu Zhongqi, "Introduction to several Neolithic cultural sites in Xinjiang", in Essays on Quaternary Geology and Glacial Geology in Xinjiang, pp. 245–24.

Not far from the site of Yuantou Mountain, it is the ancient copper mining and smelting site in Nulasai.

The ancient copper mine site of Nulasai is located three kilometers from Nileke County. The mine is located in the hillside area on the right bank of the middle reaches of the Nulasai ditch, where there is rich, high-quality crystalline pyroxene, with two mines in total. A trough-shaped depression was found on one of the mines, which was partially a large irregular pit with waste rock and ore accumulation. In this pile, ovoid stone tools up to 20 cm in diameter were recovered.[22]

On another mine passage, multiple mining holes were found. Geologists blasted a place 50 m from the top of the hill and found a dark hole. The hole is 30 m deep, 20 m long and 6 m wide at its widest point. The water at the bottom was up to 8 m deep. On the rocks at the bottom of the cave, charcoal fragments and bone fragments were found, and the bone fragments had a layer of malachite attached to them, indicating that the site was very old. The natural entrance of this shaft was not fully explored because of the waste stones and loess-like rocks covering it. Afterward, archaeologists investigated the site again. According to the report, more than ten shaft caves were found, each roughly five meters square. The cave entrances collapsed and were covered with debris, gravel and weeds. The shaft openings are connected underground, forming a network of flat mining holes and tunnels. Some of the tunnels have been flooded; but when you enter the tunnels, you can still see the pit shelves supporting the ore layers. The pit frame is made of logs wedged into the pit wall in several layers, and it is still well preserved.[23]

A large number of copper ore and stone tools were found both inside and outside of the mining shaft tunnel. Stone tools are made into round or flat stone hammers. One side is rounded, the other is slightly sharp, the largest diameter is about twenty centimeters, and they weigh three to more than ten pounds. Most of the stone hammer ends are chiseled with longitudinal and horizontal wide groove, in order to facilitate the tie with rope. The characteristics of such stone hammers are similar to that of the one found at Daye copper mining site in Hubei province, which is a site of the Warring States period. The stone hammer is considered as lifting tools for balance. The consistency of this shape provides convincing information for our analysis of the exchange of mining and metallurgical technology between the western region of Xinjiang and the Daye region of Hubei more than two thousand years ago.

The smelting site is located in a gully not far from the mine. The slag pile is one meter thick. There are wood charcoal and copper ingots within the smelting slag ash. Besides, there are pottery, ore, animal bone, etc. There are charcoal and wood fibrous marks on the black smelting slag.[24] This indicates that the ore mined in the copper

---

[22] Ibid.

[23] Mu Shunying, "Thirty Years of Archaeology in Xinjiang" Xinjiang Social Sciences, 1985, 3, p. 90.

[24] Tan'gu, "Ancient Copper Mines Discovered in Xinjiang during the Eastern Zhou Period", China Geological News, 1983, 10, 10; Wang Youbiao, "Ancient Copper Mine Sites Discovered in Nilek", Xinjiang Daily, 1984, 2, 25;, Mu Shunying and Wang MingZhe, "Ancient Ethnic Archaeological Culture in Xinjiang," Xinjiang Social Science Research, 1985, no. 6.

mine in Nulasai could be smelted by transporting it to a nearby ravine, and the fuel used for smelting was wood charcoal.

The bronze billets excavated here have been analyzed. The bronze billet is bowl shaped, round and convex on one side and flat on the other. Five pieces were found in total. The heavy ingots are heavier than ten kilograms, and light ones are between three and five kilograms each. The copper ingot block is relatively pure, copper content more than 60%. It is brittle with a silver-gray cross section, and its polished surface is silver white which can reflect.

The date of this mining site, which was taken from the supporting wood in the mine for carbon 14, was around 2440 ± 75 years ago, equivalent to the early Warring States period.[25]

From the data of the two mining and smelting sites, Yuantou Mountain and Nulasai Mountain, it seems to be concluded that mining technology, from the Spring and Autumn Period to the Warring States period, had undergone a significant development. Two different stages of technological development were marked, from surface pit mining to shaft tunnel mining. In the Warring States period, the mining technology was quite mature. Underground in the tens of meters deep, from the search for ore to digging shafts tunnels, bracket protection, mining, drainage and ventilation, extraction and transportation of ore, all require more mature technical knowledge to complete such a task. It is something that open pit mining can never be compared to.

The concentration of mining and smelting is fully in line with the principles of economy. However, it also required a tighter organization. From these data, it can be inferred that during the Warring States period, copper mining and smelting production in Xinjiang was already an important and independent production sector in society. The closely interlinked and collaborative production processes required a relatively stable production workforce with a certain level of expertise, operating under a unified schedule, in order to ensure normal production order. These data are convincing for us to understand that copper mining and smelting production in Xinjiang had been at a high level around the fourth century B.C.

Copper mining and smelting are the material bases of bronze production. To deeply understand the production of ancient bronze in Xinjiang, it is inseparable from the understanding of this foundation. Awareness and understanding of this foundation will greatly deepen our understanding of the ancient Bronze Age archaeological culture of Xinjiang.

In line with the development of copper mining and smelting during the Warring States period, more copper artifacts of this historical period were unearthed throughout Xinjiang. More bronze artifacts have been unearthed, many of which are large bronzes. In recent years, many bronzes have been unearthed in Xinyuan, Chabuchaer and Zhaosu counties in the Yili region. In Xinyuan County, in the valley of the Gongnaisi River, a number of bronze artifacts have been seen in agricultural production, including a 42-cm-high bronze warrior figurine. The warrior wears a broad-brimmed high hat with a pointed peak and a hook in front. The warrior is topless and wearing a skirt. The right leg is kneeling on the ground. Both hands are

---

[25] Carbon Dating Report V, Cultural Relics, 1984.

holding objects (broken and lost) and are placed on the legs. He has a long face, high nose, bulging tendons, which looks strong and powerful. There is also a square bronze plate with a beast squatting at each corner of the plate in an innocent manner and a bronze Fu with three animal feet. The Fu has a flat mouth and a deep bulging belly, with four ears on the upperpart, two flat and two straight and three string patterns. Other bronzes, such as the pair of tigers crouched in a circle, were broken. The two tigers have an obvious characteristic as their face and lips meet. The two beasts are bent back to each other, with silky hair rolling up, which shows a movement as a leap.[26] It is understood that during the decade of cultural revolution, in the vicinity of Xinyuan County, there has also unearthed a group of large bronze artifacts in the same style. According to those who saw the bronze, the large beast bearing bronze plate is ringed with a circle of foreign animals. The contemporary bronze also has the same beast feet and other things. In addition, in Zhaosu, Chabuchaer and other counties, large bronze Fu and beast-feet plate were also discovered. The bronze Fu is 50 cm high, and its deep belly is decorated with string pattern. The rectangular copper plate has four animal feet. In addition to the footed bronze Fu, these large bronze vessels excavated in the Yili area, from the shape of the objects and the decorative art style, are generally considered to be from the Spring and Autumn Period and the Warring States period, as the products of Saka culture which were active in Xinjiang at that time.[27] From the number of excavations, the individual shape is huge, the casting process is relatively fine, and the image of the beast is realistic and full of vigor. It fully expresses the maturity of bronze craftsmanship in this period.

In addition to the Yili area, the unearthed artifacts at the ancient tombs at the mouth of the Chabugan River in Hejing County, the eastern mouth of the Alagou, the station of Yuergou and Subashi in Shanshan County are bronzes coexisting with polychrome pottery and wooden tools in the early burials at these sites. The period is also within or before the Warring States. So, they can be regarded as the sites from this historical stage.

These materials show that the Bronze Age archaeological culture in Xinjiang had already reached a high level of development by the middle of the first millennium B.C. and even was in its heyday. After that, it gradually entered the Iron Age.

IV

Some new concepts in Xinjiang archaeological research are yet to be concretely constructed, such as the occurrence, development and transition to the Iron Age of the Bronze Age archaeological culture in Xinjiang, its own characteristics and its relationship with other regions. In this paper, even if these aspects are mentioned, at best, they are only preliminary questions. They will be tested, developed and improved in future practice.

As this paper has actually illustrated, it is possible to explore these issues of Bronze Age archaeological culture in Xinjiang on the basis of the existing archaeological

---

[26] Bayidawulieti and Guo Wenqing, "Precious cultural relics unearthed on the south bank of the Gongnaisi River," Xinjiang Art, 1984, 1.

[27] Wang Binghua, "Ancient Xinjiang Saka History", Xinjiang Social Sciences, 1985, 1.

materials and to propose some preliminary concepts. But this is only one aspect of the problem. On the other hand, as many materials are only collected and investigated, the amount of excavation materials are relatively small. This part of the excavation data is unevenly distributed, with some sites being overstudied and many areas still unstudied. Moreover, the information that has been obtained lacks in-depth analysis and research. For example, the simplest point is that most of the unearthed bronzes in the collection have not been analyzed for their metal composition, a project that should have been carried out, but there are only a few samples identified. It is not enough to make inferences about the shape and use of the objects. It goes without saying that such a situation, of course, greatly limits the depth of our understanding.

According to the available data, this paper suggests that Xinjiang already entered the Bronze Age 2000 years ago. This is, of course, a new concept. It is different from the traditional and influential concept that many scholars have traditionally and perceptively understood that "the development of ancient civilization in Xinjiang was relatively slow and far behind that of the Central Plains". This new concept, whether accurate or not, is to be tested in future archaeological practice.

From the information available so far, the shape and decoration of bronzes in Xinjiang differ greatly from those in the Yellow River Basin, and the bronzes in Xinjiang have quite distinctive characteristics of their own, while the excavations from western Central Asia and southern Siberia, such as Kazakhstan and South Altai in Russia, are being identified with more connections. This may be related to the geographical proximity to each other and the fact that in ancient times it was often the same group of inhabitants that moved in this region.

Xinjiang, as the heart of Asia, is a region of frequent ethnic migrations and is a major transportation hub. It is natural that the ancient civilizations of the Yellow River Basin cast their light and had an impact on this region. The Bronze Age archaeological culture is no exception. The Ordos bronze culture, which originated and developed in the Ordos grassland in the middle reaches of the Yellow River, and the typical Ordos-style bronze artifacts, which were also unearthed in the Hami area, are a clear and convincing example. What we have seen so far is only a point, but more information will come out as the work goes deeper. This is worthy of our attention to the study of Ordos culture, the economic and cultural links between Xinjiang and the Central Plains in ancient times and the specific ways of the links.

From a cursory observation of the bronze vessels excavated now, one impression stands out: utility vessels prevail and ritual vessels are less common. Among the utilitarian tools, the production tools (some of which are obviously related to agricultural production) account for a larger proportion. Bronze tools, of course, represent a more progressive form of productivity. Therefore, with the advent of the Bronze Age, it is worthwhile to further analyze what specific effects the use of bronze tools had on social production and socioeconomic life in Xinjiang. This is undoubtedly of great significance for the study of ancient Xinjiang history.

In this paper, I have repeatedly emphasized and repeated some generalizations about the Bronze Age archaeological culture of Xinjiang, which are very superficial. This is certainly not a modest statement, but a limitation that is inevitable at this stage. In this case, I publicly present these views in the hope of not only promoting deeper research, but also to receive help and correction from various parties. We hope that with the joint efforts of all parties, the research will continue to develop and improve, and that the archaeological research in Xinjiang will further prosper.

Chapter 3
Relative Analogies in the Ritual Use of Red Mineral Pigments (Ochre, Hematite) in Neolithic and Eneolithic Burials from Xinjiang and Bulgaria

Maria Marinova

Abstract The practice of sprinkling red pigments on the body, colouring individual parts of it or burying red objects with the dead as part of the funeral rite was well known to much of the prehistoric world. It has also been attested in a number of burials from the 7th to 2nd millennium B.C. in China, particularly in Xinjiang. This article presents examples from the most ancient documented burial practices with red ochre coloration in the Bulgarian lands of the Neolithic (6300–4900 B.C.) and the Eneolithic (4900–4100 B.C.) periods, with the aim of drawing relative analogies from culturally close prehistoric contexts. Such relative analogies could outline new perspectives on the interpretation of the symbolic use of red mineral pigments (hematite, red ochre) in prehistoric burials in Xinjiang and could also potentially illuminate their ritual and social logic. The research presented here also outlines some of the main modern hypotheses that have been proposed in regard to the practical and semantic role of red pigments in mortuary context. In addition, a linguistic observation of the author concerning the culturally significant etymology of the word *"man"* in Semitic languages is put forward, which might have preserved primary connotations underlying the eschatological association of red ochre or other red-coloured attributes with life, vital energy and the transformation of inanimate matter into living matter.

Keywords Prehistoric burials · Red ochre · Hematite · Ritual use · Xinjiang · Bulgaria · Neolithic · Eneolithic

3.1 Introduction

Colours are unique historical record left to us by our ancestors, which, passing through space and time, conveys important information about their aesthetic pursuits,

---

M. Marinova (✉)
Faculty of Modern and Classical Philology, Department of Chinese Studies, Sofia University "St. Kliment Ochridski", Sofia, Bulgaria
e-mail: mtmarinova@uni-sofia.bg

worldview and social archetypes. Hence, the multifarious role of colours in ancient societies is enjoying growing academic interest, and they are viewed as essential pieces in solving the puzzle of the material and spiritual lifestyle of early humans. The means of expression of prehistoric artists were strongly limited by the available resources and technologies for pigment processing, and perhaps this accounts for the scarcity of shades in Palaeolithic art, which employed just three main colours: red, white and black. It is possible that only mineral pigments have survived until the present day due to their durability, which enables them to be well preserved in the archaeological record, while most colourants based on organic material extracted from plants or animals (except charcoal, which was used for black colouration) were lost over the course of thousands of years.

It is generally accepted that each colour in this triad had its own importance and symbolism, conditioned by the cosmological, mythical and religious ideas of the bearers of ancient archaeological cultures. The primary layer of their symbolic meaning usually includes semiotic associations of colours such as: white—purity; red—blood, fire; black—earth, darkness; yellow—sun, gold; blue—water, sea and so on. But the situational use of colours in specific social contexts must also be taken into account, in such cases we have a secondary charge with connotations and meanings of the objects—mediators, as well as of the applied colours themselves (Izdimirski 2017: 423).

The first colourants are known from Old Palaeolithic contexts, and researchers determine their collection and use as one of the indicators for the development of symbolic and abstract thinking in ancient groups. Although the Middle Palaeolithic witnessed the evolution of both social formations and the utilization of pigments, the polyfunctional role and potential of the latter found full expression in the rock art and the funeral rituals of the Upper Palaeolithic (Petru 2006: 204).

Grave complexes are one of the many groups of monuments that allow us to gain understanding of the spiritual life of early hunter-gatherer societies. Identification and analysis of the role of pigments in the burial practices of ancient human populations constitutes an essential aspect of the interpretation of funeral rites, the restoration of their symbolic architecture and the underlying religious and mythological notions. One of the first pigments, known and used by humans from the very dawn of civilization, is red ochre. In its natural state, the mineral has a yellow or orange to reddish colour, which becomes red when dehydrated at high temperature. Red ochre is a mineral pigment, which is derived from four basic types of iron ores—hematite, limonite, siderite and magnetite, of which hematite is most frequently found in geological and soil formations. The wide geographical distribution and utilization of red ochre is due to the fact that hematite deposits are contained nearly universally throughout the rock strata and are common in Europe, Australia, the Middle East and North America (Stafford et al. 2003: 82).

The spatial and temporal distribution of the prehistoric groups who used ochre in mortuary contexts is also extremely wide. The practice of sprinkling red ochre on the body, colouring individual parts of it, or burying red ochre with the dead, occurs in different cultures with varying frequency. Even if we assume that it originated sporadically and simultaneously in remote parts of the world, its intrusive presence as an element of the burial rituals of prehistoric cultures and the observed patterns in its use suggest that some of the properties of red ochre were permanently associated with the transition from life to death, and these associations developed in later epochs.

One of the greatest drawbacks in the study of red mineral pigments in prehistory is the lack of a narrow definition to be applied in the description and analysis of the archaeological record, which leads to a certain amount of ambiguity regarding the use of the terms "ochre", "red pigment", "hematite" and "iron oxide" in archaeological contexts. Almost half a decade ago, Häusler (1980: 636) notes that the term "ochre" is often used in scientific literature as a most general term designating red or reddish colourant. Despite appeals for greater specification in the recording of archaeological finds of pigments, this trend still continues. Additionally, Butzer (1980: 635) points out that since red pigment can be obtained by processing hematite, limonite and ferruginized sandstones, "ochre" may be such a generic term as to be misleading.

In this article, the author adheres as much as possible to the terminology used in the cited excavation reports or scientific articles, and where the word "ochre" is used in the broadest sense, it should be understood as "the red pigment obtained from iron ore or organic mineral soil formations that contain iron oxides and have undergone thermal or mechanical treatment and which can be used in their pure form or as a component in composite materials, giving them colour or other properties" (Kosinskaja et al. 2016: 376). The collective term "red mineral pigments" in the context of this research paper should be considered to denote any of the following colourants: red ochre, hematite, iron oxide and cinnabar.

3.2 Ritual Use of Red Mineral Pigments in Prehistoric China Against a Global Background

A large amount of scientific literature is devoted to tracing, describing, analysing and interpreting the role of red mineral pigments in the ontological paradigm of ancient cultures around the world. The first traces of ochre use are associated with human industries in Kenya as far back as the time of *Homo erectus*, about 285,000 years ago, long before its metallurgic properties were discovered (Schmandt-Besserat 1980: 143). The oldest iron oxide finds in Europe that constitute the earliest documented implementation of red ochre by Neanderthals are retrieved during excavations in the Netherlands and are dated to 200–250,000 years ago (Roebroeks et al. 2012: 1889), which is contemporary to the early ochre use in the African record.[1] The utilization of iron oxides by Late Pleistocene Neanderthals in Europe is also well attested, especially for the period 60–40,000 years BP.[2] The ritual use of ochre on the

---

[1] See Henshilwood et al. (2009), Jacobs et al. (2006).
[2] For overview see d'Errico et al. (2010: 3100).

continent in mortuary contexts[3] continued into the Mesolithic and has been found in sites in Denmark, Sweden and France (Jones and MacGregor 2002: 8). The advance towards Neolithic and Eneolithic times did not mark the end of this custom, as evidenced by numerous burials in Central and Eastern Europe (Lenneis 2007: 131), some of which will be discussed in greater detail in the course of this article.

Use of ochre/hematite in funeral environments is well attested in almost every corner of the prehistoric world, in most cases as powdered element sprinkled on the skeleton or the skull of the tomb owner, or sometimes in the form of lumps spread around the body. A quick look at the research material on the subject reveals that its presence in a mortuary context is documented in the Levant, the Near East, North and South Africa, pre-Columbian America, Malta, Siberia, Russia, Australia, South America, Iran, Pakistan and many other locations around the globe, thus turning it into a universal phenomenon intertwined in the concepts of life and death of ancient societies.

China's archaeology, developing at the pace of the economic growth of the country in the new century, is constantly producing new valuable discoveries that build on and expand the paradigms about the earliest history of this vast region. The symbolic significance of iron oxides/ochre/hematite and cinnabar in the rites of the Palaeolithic, Neolithic and early Bronze Age societies on the territory of China[4] is also well attested by numerous finds. Hematite powder (赭石粉末), pieces of red hematite, stone beads and 25 animal teeth coloured by red hematite were found among the human fossils of an intentional burial at Zhoukoudian Upper cave (周口店山顶洞遗址)[5] (Gao 2008: 733), indicating that by the Late Palaeolithic, a complex suite of spiritual beliefs and rituals had begun to develop in North China.[6] Other important sites where ritual use of hematite powder or other unidentified red pigments in a funeral context is documented include the Early Neolithic site Donghulin (东胡林遗址) in Beijing, the Neolithic sites Beiqiu (贝丘遗址) and Changtang (长塘遗址) in the Guangxi Zhuang Autonomous Region and the Bronze Age culture Kayue (卡约文化) in Qinghai province (Gao 2011: 102). Presence of red ochre (赤铁矿) is also attested in Neolithic and early Bronze Age burials from the Qijia culture

---

[3] Wreschner et al. (1980: 632) suggests, that with the appearance of *Homo sapiens sapiens* in Europe, there is a significant temporal and spatial expansion of ochre customs. In the Upper Palaeolithic, ochre becomes more frequent grave good (Riel-Salvatore and Clark 2001: 454–457) and its symbolic-ritual connotations develop. The Upper Palaeolithic also marks a time of increase in the number of caches of ochre, mortars and grinders for ochre preparation, and accumulations of ochre-processing debris in occupation areas (Schmandt-Besserat 1980: 144), which is significant of the important role that ochre played in the life and the spiritual culture of the then society. The observed similarities in ochre practices between Palaeolithic groups (in Wreschner et al. 1980: 631) have also become a factor in the debate over the origins and dispersion of cultures, although the proposed hypotheses regarding the derivation of one culture from another still remain highly speculative.

[4] For a survey of the geographical distribution of red mineral pigments in China, see: Tian (2018: 26–29).

[5] The Upper Cave was discovered in 1930 and excavated in 1933–24.

[6] For an overview of the emergence and evolution of early modern humans in China, see: Liu 2013: 235–244.

(齐家文化) of the Upper Yellow River Valley (Chen 2013: 111; Mai et al. 2016: 6) and the Dawenkou culture (大汶口文化), which flourished in the Lower Yellow River and the Huai River Basin areas (Luan 2013: 418).

Another red pigment associated with inhumation rituals in China, as well as in other parts of the world, is cinnabar (朱砂), although it is usually found less often in the archaeological record.[7] Traces of cinnabar in graves from the Bronze Age culture Sanxingdui (三星堆文化) in the Sichuan Basin and the Xipo cemetery (西坡墓地) of the Miaodigou (庙底沟) period of the Yangshao culture (仰韶文化) in Henan province have also been observed (Sun 2013: 155; Li 2013: 222). There is evidence that pulverized cinnabar was spread around the skull of the dead and over the bottom of a wooden coffin in a medium-size burial at the Zhouli site (妯娌遗址) of the early Longshan culture (龙山文化) in central Henan province, which in combination with other grave attributes is interpreted as a higher social status marker in a stratified society (Zhao 2013: 238).

The archaeological excavations of the Erlitou site (二里头遗址), dated to 1800–1500 B.C., revealed that high-ranking individuals were buried in large graves, containing not only bronze drinking vessels and jade ritual objects, but also wooden coffins with traces of cinnabar (Xu 2013: 314). Thus, the red pigment was considered to be an attribute of elite burials from Bronze Age China bearing special religious significance (Xu 2013: 314). Cinnabar as an indicator of high status in the social hierarchy is also documented in burials from the early Shang era (Yuan 2013: 333). Moreover, it was employed as a pigment for inscribing various characters such as numbers, human- and animal-like symbols and pictographs on the ceramic jars, excavated from sacrificial pits from this period (Yuan 2013: 339). Therefore, the presence of this colourant in the sophisticated ceremonial activities that were essential to theocracy during the early Shang period can be seen as an important social marker, loaded with profound ritual semantics at the same time.[8]

3.3 Red Colourants and Red Objects in Prehistoric Burials from Xinjiang

Northwest China's Xinjiang Uyghur Autonomous Region, with its vast territory of over 1.6 million square kilometres, is a real archaeological treasury, which has preserved in its depths evidence of the interactions of the ancient societies. As a complex contact zone between the East and the West, its abundant prehistory continues to be the subject of active scientific interest[9] and academic dialogue, and

---

[7] Cinnabar (mercury sulphide ore) is a more rarely seen alternative to ochre in prehistoric burials. Although harder than ochre, it can still be crushed to a powder and mixed with water to make red liquid with a fresh look, whereas ochre always has brownish hue (Clifford 2012: 237).

[8] For detailed analysis of cinnabar use in funeral context see Gao (2011: 104).

[9] For an overview of prehistoric archaeological research in Xinjiang, see Derevianko et al. (2012: 3–5).

each new discovery quickly becomes a factor in shaping the early picture of the region. Until recently, it was considered that the Palaeolithic period in this dry arid region was relatively underrepresented and that most Palaeolithic sites discovered in Xinjiang were "unstratified surface lag aggregates of artefacts" (Derevianko et al. 2012: 5). That is why the first Palaeolithic site in Xinjiang—the Tongtiandong cave site (通天洞遗址) in Jeminay County (吉木乃县), which was excavated in 2016–2017, made a real sensation and was distinguished as one of China's six greatest archaeological discoveries of 2017. The cultural deposits of the cave contained more than 2000 pieces of fossils, stone tools, bronzeware and ironware dating back 3500–45,000 years (Yu 2018: 132–135), but no traces of red ochre or hematite have been reported in the excavation accounts.

Evidence for the ritual use of red mineral pigments by early inhabitants of Xinjiang comes from two Eneolithic tombs in Hoboskar County in Tacheng Prefecture (塔城地区和布克赛尔县)—in one case hematite powder was sprinkled on the right side of the skull, and in the other case on the skeleton (Wang et al. 2018: 129). Large pieces of hematite were also found on the east side of the foot of the dead in Eneolithic grave M9 from the Huojierte cemetery in Emin County (额敏霍吉尔特墓地), dated 2920–2750 B.C. (Wang et al. 2018:129).

In graves M21 and M22 of Ayituohan No. 1 cemetery (阿依托汗一号墓地) in Habahe County, the skeletal remains of a total of three adult individuals abundantly sprinkled with "red colourant" were discovered, and their age was determined as 4500 years BP (Li 2018: 105). Excavation reports reveal that the physical type of the tomb owners displays Indo-European racial affiliations, and DNA analysis confirms their western Eurasian origin (Li 2018: 106). According to the typological characteristics of the burials, Chinese researchers unequivocally determine the two graves as "remnants of the Afanasievo culture on the territory of Xinjiang" (Li 2018: 105–106).

In fact, ritual use of hematite or red ochre in Xinjiang prehistory is often associated with burials, which are believed to follow the structure and the ritual system of the Afanasievo or Andronovo culture. Thus, the group of 31 Bronze Age tombs in Shihuyao village near the city of Shihezi (石河子十户窑墓群), whose burial chambers were reportedly covered with ochre—a distinctive feature of Andronovo type burials—are considered to be an emblematic example in this respect (Wang et al. 2018: 130).

The Xiaohe cemetery (小河墓地), displaying a unique and advanced culture 3500 years ago, is another important Bronze Age site in Xinjiang, which is considered to have been influenced by the Afanasievo culture. Among the numerous red painted relics discovered in the graves (including wooden pillars, ox horns, arrow heads) (XWKYS 2004: 340–367), it is worth mentioning the red cosmetic sticks covered with hematite powder, which were contained in leather bags, placed next to the waist of most female mummies, and which probably served for painting of the red lines found on the forehead of many of the bodies (Mai et al. 2016: 2).

In grave M2 of the Xiaohe cemetery, a unique wooden human-sized idol was discovered buried in a coffin, wrapped in three layers of calfskin. On top of the coffin a number of tiny, untreated tamarisk twigs (红柳枝) were placed (Liu 2008: 88). Such twigs were also found on the coffin in grave M4, and some of the other burials produced a bouquet of tamarisk twigs, as well as tamarisk sticks (红柳棍) engraved with characters (XWKYS 2004: 340–367). Grave M21 of the Yanhai cemetery in Shanshan County (鄯善洋海墓地), which has been dated to 12–8th century B.C., yielded a similar find—tiny tamarisk sticks, placed on a wooden funeral bed (Li et al. 2011: 112). The documented use of reddish tamarisk twigs as part of the burial inventory, although sporadic, seems to follow a certain pattern and displays apparent symbolic characteristics. This symbolism can be associated either with the material (wood) or the colour (red) of the tamarisk, or with some other abstract connotation, but the way the twigs are dispersed on the coffin or on the funeral bed is very reminiscent of the way the lumps of ochre are scattered around the body, as attested in other burials. It is possible that tamarisk twigs or other natural red objects played the role of substitutes in areas where hematite ore or other red mineral pigments were not available—a presumption which deserves to be more systematically studied and analysed in relation to the overall archaeological context of the region.

3.4 Red Mineral Pigments as Part of the Neolithic and Eneolithic Burials Practices in Bulgaria

In its search for correct interpretation of a particular element or complex of elements, archaeology often takes advantage of auxiliary tools such as the relative analogies drawn from culturally close prehistoric contexts that could show new perspectives of analysis and illuminate the ritual and social logic of certain phenomena. With this aim, the author will present archaeological data related to the use of red mineral pigments from the most ancient documented burial practices in the Bulgarian lands of the Neolithic (6300/6100 B.C.–4900/4850 B.C.) and the Eneolithic period (4900/4850–4100/3800 B.C.). Much of the data comes from large grave complexes that have been used systematically for centuries, which provides a chance to trace the development of certain characteristics and to demonstrate that the burial rite is not a "statistical set"[10] of typological and cultural features, but rather a "complex evolving system with several levels".[11]

Like Xinjiang, the Balkan Peninsula has also been a crossroads of cultures since ancient times, but moreover, the cradle of an ancient progressive civilization with strong influence since the Neolithic. It is widely accepted that the study of the prehistory of today's Bulgarian lands plays a key role in understanding the principles and trends in the development of the Neolithic, Eneolithic and Bronze Age cultures (i.e. the period from the end of the 7th to the 2nd millennium B.C.) throughout the entire Southeast Europe. In the perceptions of the earliest farmers and pastoralists in this region, the world of the living and the dead was united, and it was because of this

---

[10] See origin and interpretation of the concept in: Gening and Borzunov (1975: 44).

[11] See origin and interpretation of the concept in: Korenjako (1977: 5–7).

idea that most Neolithic inhabitants[12] of the Bulgarian lands were buried within the settlement of the living (under the floor of the house or near the house)—an act that unequivocally testifies to their immortal role in the life of the ancient society (Nikolov 2003: 9–10).

The analysis of Neolithic burial complexes[13] from the Bulgarian lands shows that, as a general rule, burial inventory is relatively rare and is found in only 26% of the graves, but its presence has a certain symbolic role (Bachvarov 2003: 133). Grave inventory is usually associated with the social status of the dead and includes jewellery (beads, decorative needles, anthropomorphic figurines), ceramic vessels (that probably contained food and drink at the time of burial), animal bones and seashells, ceramic, flint and stone tools (awls), unprocessed stones (including lumps of ochre or other types of red stones), fragments of ceramic vessels, etc.

For this Eurasian region in broader terms, sprinkling with red ochre is registered in the Levant as early as the Natufian culture (12,500–9500 B.C.) and is also known from Early Neolithic tombs from Central Anatolia,[14] where it continued to exist during the Late Neolithic and the Early Eneolithic period (Bachvarov 2003: 247). Although sporadically, both from a chronological and a territorial point of view, the spread of this custom in Southeast Europe covers the entire Neolithic Age. In a burial context, red ochre is mainly found in northeast Bulgaria, the Rhodope Mountains, the Sofia Valley, Transylvania, the Tisza valley, Muntenia and Banat. Archaeologists believe that this Neolithic practice in Southeast Europe and Anatolia most likely developed from local Epipalaeolithic traditions (Bachvarov 2003: 146, 247).

Traces of red ochre have been registered in three Early Neolithic complexes in Bulgaria, where two of the graves contained the skeletal remains of children, and the third one—of a woman. In one case, the marks of the red pigment were found on the femurs, while in the other two, pieces of ochre were sprinkled over the skeleton (Bachvarov 2003: 145). In an early Neolithic tomb of a child from Kardzhali (in southeast Bulgaria), a small red stone was discovered in the right hand of the deceased, and similar finds[15] have been witnessed in earlier South European cultures—ochre-painted stones were also documented in Epigravetic sites in Italy and in the Mesolithic culture Vlasac in Serbia (Bachvarov 2003: 109, 137). Red ochre was also registered

---

[12] Archaeologists estimate that the human bones of only about 10% of the Neolithic population of the Balkans have been discovered. The skeletal remains of a large part of the Neolithic inhabitants are missing not only in the Bulgarian lands, but also in the entire early agricultural ekumene—from the Middle East to the Atlantic (Nikolov 2003: 10).

[13] More than 150 Neolithic burials have been discovered within the relatively small territory of Bulgaria (approximately 111,000 km^2).

[14] The foreheads of the dead from the early Neolithic settlement of Çatalhöyük in Anatolia were painted with red ochre—a ritual that was interpreted as a sign of high social status of the tomb owner (Mellaart 1975: 102).

[15] During rescue archeological excavations of burials from the Early Bronze Age in the Yambol region (southeast Bulgaria), skeletal remains of adults and children, whose bones were abundantly sprinkled with ochre were discovered, and in one case a small bronze awl and a small unprocessed jasper were placed as burial gifts (Bakardzhiev 2005a: 82, 2005b: 151).

in 7 of the 28 burials from the late Neolithic cemetery near the village of Golyamo Delchevo in northeast Bulgaria (Zanotti 1984/1985: 81).

The advance of the Eneolithic period witnessed some innovations in the mortuary concepts and practices of the Balkan population: the majority of the dead in the second half of the 5th millennium B.C. were buried in necropolises outside the settlements in individual burial pits by bone placement in anatomical order and accompanied by a standard set of grave inventory (Stavreva 2018: 117). The excavation of more than 1200 burials in the necropolis near the village of Durankulak,[16] covering a time span of a millennium, provided an excellent chance to trace the evolution of the burial practices of the Late Neolithic and the successive Eneolithic community of the Hamangia culture[17] in the Danube delta region (Boyadziev 2008: 85). The analysis of the tombs revealed that in the period between 5500–4600 B.C., the arrangement of grave goods did not follow any strict rules, and they could be situated around and/or upon the whole body, which applied especially to the teeth of grazing animals and the sherds of storage vessels that were often found scattered around the skeleton (Boyadziev 2008: 87). By the end of this period, major transformations in the contents of the burial gifts took place and their layout in the grave also began to follow certain rules: the vessels were placed mainly around or behind the head of the deceased, or next to or upon the chest (Boyadziev 2008: 87).

At the end of its development, the Hamangia culture gradually evolved into the late Eneolithic culture of Varna (4450–4150 B.C.[18]), which was characterized by profound social, spiritual and to a certain extent ethnical transformations and further standardization of the burial rituals (Boyadziev 2008: 91). Although the basic elements of the rites (burial features, alignment of the body, treatment of the body, and arrangement of the grave goods) were preserved, most of them were reconsidered in the process of internal development of the community, and eventually crystallized into a set of mortuary practices with strong local characteristics (Boyadzhiev 2008: 90).

The excavations of the Durankulak necropolis revealed that symbolic burials ("cenotaphs") were practiced from the very beginning of the Hamangia culture and continued throughout all its phases. Symbolic burials were performed in grave pits supplied with burial goods, identical to the ones that contained inhumations, but without any evidence for human bodies (Boyadziev 2008: 86, 89). Like in normal burials, the grave goods in cenotaphs were clustered mostly in the northern part of the burial chamber, where the head of the deceased was usually placed (Boyadziev 2008: 90). The use of red ochre in the Durankulak necropolis was documented in 14 out of the 440 Late Eneolithic graves, and in 12 of the cases ochre colouration was

---

[16] Situated at the Black Sea coast, near the Romania-Bulgaria border.

[17] The Hamangia culture is an archaeological culture of settled agricultural tribes from the late Neolithic age, which flourished in 5500–4600 B.C. on the territory of southeast Romania and northeast Bulgaria, between the lower reaches of the Danube River and the Black Sea.

[18] The author follows the dating of the Eneolithic cultures in Bulgaria, proposed by Todorova (2003: 276–290).

observed on the skeletal remains of females (Stavreva 2018: 118), thus marking a strong sex differentiation in its use by the local community.

Over 1200 Late Eneolithic burials, located in 31 archaeological complexes, have been discovered on the territory of Bulgaria so far. Most of them are necropolises, but about 150 are found in a settlement environment (Stavreva 2018: 116). Among them, the discovery and excavation of the rich necropolis near the city of Varna in 1972–1991, revealing the existence of a spiritually and technologically advanced civilization, became an epoch-making event for the most ancient history of mankind as a whole. The abundant and diverse finds[19] radically changed the concepts of global archaeological and historical science about the prehistoric society in the Balkans and in Europe during the 5th millennium B.C., by proving the existence of a well-organized community with social differentiation and a ruling elite of priest-chiefs (Minchev 2008: 9). The necropolis occupies an area of 7500 m^2 and is comprised of 294 graves from the Eneolithic period, 43 of which are considered to be symbolic burials (Higham et al. 2008: 95). Some of these cenotaph graves contained clay masks with gold objects placed strategically on the location of eyes, mouth, nose and ears (Higham et al. 2008: 95). The original excavation reports describe yellow and/or red ochre in the majority of the burials from the Varna necropolis, without providing exact numbers (Zanotti 1984/1985), and red ochre was also registered in seven of the cenotaphs (Stavreva 2018: 118), thus confirming its important mystical role in the funerary customs of the region.

It should be noted that ochre has been documented in some of the richest Late Eneolithic graves from Bulgaria and was probably incorporated as a mandatory element of sophisticated burial rituals performed for high-ranking individuals. Red ochre covered the bottom of the emblematic grave No. 43 in the Varna necropolis, which belonged to a high-status person with royal insignia (Stavreva 2018: 118) and contained more gold than has been found in other archaeological sites from that period in the rest of the world. A thick layer of red ochre, located beneath the pots placed above the head of the dead, was also documented in the richest grave No. 18 in the Devnya necropolis, which also contained a lot of inventory, golden ornaments and copper tools, and was interpreted as the burial of a chief (Stavreva 2018: 118).

From the above examples, it can be concluded that the ritual use of red mineral pigments in the funeral rites in the Bulgarian lands was well known as early as the Neolithic, but the fact that it is registered in a relatively small number of burials from different parts of the country suggests that during this period its use was selective and did not follow strictly defined rules. By analogy with Xinjiang tamarisk twigs, it is possible that in prehistoric burials in Southeast Europe, jasper or another red mineral or red-coloured stone played an allegorical role identical to that of red mineral pigments, with possible symbolic connotations discussed below. The mass use of

---

[19] The finds from the Varna necropolis include over 3000 golden objects with various design and with a total weight of more than 6 kg, 160 copper objects, over 230 flint artifacts, about 90 stone objects, and more than 650 clay products, as well as over 12,000 Dentalium shells and about 1100 imported Spondylus shell ornaments (bracelets, necklaces and appliques) (Higham et al. 2008: 95). The golden ornaments from the Varna necropolis were dated to the 5th millennium B.C., and were therefore the earliest evidence of goldwork in the world.

red mineral pigments in the burials of the Varna Chalcolithic necropolis suggests the development of its ritual function and its transformation into a mandatory element of the burial practices of the Black Sea civilization in northeast Bulgaria. Its presence both in cenotaphs and in the graves of social leaders confirms its great symbolic capacity and probably powerful magical function.

Important information about ancient funeral practices can also be obtained from the textiles used in burials, the colours of which have also been regarded as socially significant. Fabrics were used not only for the ritual clothing of the deceased on his/her last journey to the afterlife, but also for wrapping/covering items of the grave inventory, as a bedcover or blanket for the dead, and as decoration for parts of the interior of the tomb (Izdimirski 2017: 425). The most ancient textile remains on the territory of Bulgaria have been recovered from the Eneolithic necropolises near Durankulak, Devnya and Varna, and were coloured mainly in red. They are discovered both in graves with inhumation as well as in symbolic graves, while remnants of black and white textiles are documented much less frequently (Petrova 2006: 30, 34). In 22 burials from the Eneolithic necropolis near the village of Durankulak, on the skeletons or at the bottom of the grave pits, traces/imprints of clothes coloured with red ochre were found, and on the foreheads of nine skulls traces of red stripe imprints were observed (Avramova 2008: 23). Since the coloured clothes were discovered in graves with more abundant and diverse inventory, it is supposed that their owners were of higher social status (Avramova 2008: 23). The use of red/purple fabrics as part of the burial rituals of rich Thracian and Hellenistic burials from the middle of the first millennium B.C. is also well documented (Izdimirski 2017: 427–433).

3.4.1 Multi-layered Semantics of Red Mineral Pigments in a Mortuary Context

Reconstruction of the burial rites of early societies is a complex process with a large degree of hypotheticality, as many factors that accompany inhumation and are integral elements of the funeral rite (such as the verbal and nonverbal rituals) as a general rule remain archaeologically elusive. Thus, prehistoric archaeology is placed in a position where on the basis of partial material remains, it should be able to interpret phenomena of an immeasurably larger scale. That is why the interdisciplinary approach and the methods of integrated science are required for the accomplishment of this elaborate task.

According to Aleshkin (1981: 3) "the standard (traditional) burial rite of any archaeological culture" consists of two interrelated components, the first of which characterizes the ritual side and includes traditionally approved ritual actions before, during and after the burial, while the second one characterizes the social position of the dead and comprises the material elements of the funeral rite—burial facility, grave inventory and burial posture. Due to its multi-layered semantics and function, the use of red ochre or other red colourant in prehistoric burials can be related to any of the above two components. Taking into account the wide spatial and geographical distribution of red mineral pigments, the interpretation of their specific role in a particular archaeological, cultural or temporal context should be combined with analysis of the other elements that constitute it, and not isolated. Since this article does not aim to perform an in-depth research of the characteristics of red colourants for a defined archaeological culture, but rather aims to broaden the scope and provide new start points of interpretation, only some of the main modern hypotheses that have been proposed in regard to the practical and semantical role of red ochre/hematite in prehistoric burials will be outlined.[20]

The use of red mineral pigments in Palaeolithic cave art marked the social and cultural development of the early human societies, and its presence in intentional burials from this period is regarded as an indication of their important role in the Palaeolithic belief system. Petru (2006: 206) suggests a powerful symbolic relation between ochre and femininity in the Upper Palaeolithic, since many Palaeolithic Venus figurines were painted with red ochre or hematite, perhaps also as a symbol of transformation of the female body during pregnancy.

In opposition to the predominant symbolic approach towards the study of red pigments' utilization by early man, Nicolau (2016: 188) proposes a double use of red ochre—functional and symbolic—as a driving force for its wide dissemination in contextual, chronological and geographical sense, and as an explanation of its "practical omnipresence" during prehistory. Through the methods of modern experimental archaeology, some of the most prominent practical uses of iron oxide in Prehistory have been proved, such as its implementation as a tanning and preserving agent for leather and food, as a filler which reinforces the adhesive capacities of other adherent substances, as a medicinal substance with astringent, antiseptic, deodorizing, soothing and healing properties, as an insect repellent, as an abrasive, as a waterproofing agent for wood, etc. (Nicolau 2016: 190–193; Roebroeks et al. 2012: 1889; Velo 1984: 674; d'Errico et al. 2010: 3100; Rifkin 2011, 2012). The purely utilitarian properties of red mineral pigments in ancient societies are also confirmed by the fact that hematite and ochre have also been recovered from sites where there were no traces of symbolic activity, such as quarries.[21]

But it should be kept in mind that most objects from the material culture of early civilizations had both a utilitarian function and a symbolic meaning, probably derived from their functionality and expressed as an abstract value or artistic potential.[22] That

---

[20] For an overview of older opinions on red ochre symbolic meanings and connotations, see Wreschner et al. (1980: 631).

[21] Prehistoric quarries have produced an abundance of information regarding methods for the procurement of ochre and ancient technologies for its processing. See Stafford et al. (2003: 86–88).

[22] Nicolau (2016: 205–206) proposes the hypothesis that the evolution of symbolic meaning is a complex process which undergoes three phases: (1) Phase 1: apprehension of the elementary properties of certain agents/natural elements and establishment of fixed definition patterns; (2) Phase 2: regionalization, which includes lexicalization of the meaning of the application of the substance and its adaptation to the needs of the community that created it; (3) Phase 3: development phase during which, the meanings derived from said lexicalization begin to integrate into the cosmogony of the group.

is why the most incontestable facet of the use of red mineral colourants in prehistory is their symbolic function, which has been verified by numerous evidence. Since the Neolithic, iron oxides have been employed as pigments for rock paintings and pottery decorations, for colouring fabrics and clothing, as well as for painting or drawing on the floor or the walls of buildings. It is probable that they were also used as colourants for perishable materials such as bark, wood, leather, basketry and vegetal fibres that did not survive in the archaeological record (Schmandt-Besserat 1980: 144). Another aesthetic or abstract application of red ochre is its use as body paint—a practice that continued among many groups well into the historic period. Therefore, as Wadley (2005: 589) affirms, the ritual and the functional use of red ochre should not be opposed, but rather should be treated as complementary to each other.

The varied symbolic meanings of red pigments in a burial context have also evolved as their contextual uses became more diverse and complex. Red ochre has been traditionally associated with blood since the early twentieth century, and in many spiritual teachings, blood is recognized as the carrier of vital energy. This association is reinforced not only by the etymology of the ancient Greek word "hematite" ("blood stone"), but also by the documented use of iron oxides in fertility and life/death rituals, common among current hunter-gatherers.[23] Another support of this presumption is the healing effect of ochre as a medicine that stops bleeding and cures snake bites, which is well known today among some African tribes, and in this sense the pigment may have been perceived as a revitalizing agent in general. Stavreva (2018: 120) supposes that because of its association with blood, red ochre was taken as a tool, which, as the life-giving fluid, would empower the soul of the dead to start a new life in the afterlife.[24] As part of the funerary inventory, red ochre/hematite was also loaded with apotropaic connotations and perceived as a magical substance that, in the afterlife, could safeguard the most vulnerable members of the society, such as young women and children (Bachvarov 2003: 146), or ward off evil spirits and protect the object or the body decorated with it (Mellaart 1967: 149–150).

Petru (2006: 206) argues that ochre was used in funeral rites as a symbol of transformation and that together with the whiteness of bones and the blackness of the grave, red was part of the mighty tricolour scheme that symbolized death. Red ochre is associated with fire through the process of acquiring its colour when heated, and since fire itself is also an important agent of transformation (it could change the temperature and the properties of an object), red pigment signifies the transformation of the soul to another reality and is interpreted as an aid to its realization (Petru 2006: 204–206; Stavreva 2018: 120). It should be noted that the foetal position of the body, observed in many prehistoric burials, can also be seen as an expression of the idea of rebirth in a divine realm. This concept is particularly well developed by the Thracian civilization in the Bulgarian lands (2nd millennium B.C.–sixth century AD), who

---

[23] See in Wreschner et al. (1980).

[24] According to Eliade (1978: 9), the use of red ochre is proof of belief in the afterlife, and ancient people perceived it as "a ritual substitute for blood, hence a symbol of life".

considered death as a process of transition from profane to sacred existence, and enriched it with positive connotations.

Despite its long existence, red ochre has not yet left the historical scene and its multi-layered functions continue to flourish in some societies, such as among the indigenous population of Australia. The surviving oral and written records of the Australian Aboriginal peoples have preserved a complex mythological context (Jones 2019: 351–357), which validates the divine properties of this substance and confirms its status as an indispensable element of the lifestyle, the religious practices and the economy of the community. Red ochre as a fundamental part of the spiritual life of other communities, such as the African Ndembu, the Yemeni Jews, the South African Kings, the Saharan Tuaregs and Yamana (a hunter-gatherer people of Tierra del Fuego) has also been well documented (Knight et al. 1995: 95; Wadley 2005: 588; Nicolau 2016: 201), thus reflecting a complex system of cultural beliefs that may have its historical roots.

3.5 Conclusion

The author has conducted this preliminary research of documented use of red ochre and hematite in prehistoric burials from Xinjiang and the Balkan Peninsula as an attempt to derive points of contact or common features. As in the reconstruction of proto-languages, where the relationship between different language groups is evidenced not only by direct comparisons, but also by investigation of the evolutionary processes in them, so the genetic link between remote archaeological cultures can also be indirectly verified by the discovery of a common source of certain archetypes. The given examples show that the properties of red ochre and hematite were known to prehistoric societies in China as early as the Palaeolithic and Neolithic, and their semantics and ritual role in the funeral customs probably gradually expanded with time to denote everything divine, magical and sacred by the time of the Shang dynasty. For the territory of Xinjiang, it is considered that the red mineral pigments in the early burials, together with other typological characteristics, were introduced by the Afanasievo culture as the most direct source of influence in the region. We should not rule out, however, the possibility that many of the features attributed to the Afanasievo culture were actually shared by a wide range of neighbouring cultures across Eurasia and may have another, much earlier prototype, which for a number of reasons has been excluded a priori as a formative factor. For a very long time the archaeological data from the Balkan Peninsula—the cradle of European civilization—has been vastly neglected in the research and reconstruction of Eurasian prehistory and its role in shaping the early picture of the continent may have been largely under-appreciated.

In addition, the author would like to conclude this article with an interesting linguistic observation in regard to the semantic layers of red ochre.

Quite often, in search of the religious-symbolic logic of archaeologically attested elements of the spiritual life of prehistoric societies, science seeks support in mythic narratives or scriptures that have preserved certain basic paradigms. As discussed, the primary associations of ochre/hematite or other red objects used in a mortuary context have always gravitated around blood, life, transformation, rebirth, etc., and some of these associations certainly date back to the dawn of human civilization. Is it a coincidence, then, that in the biblical record of the name of the first man on earth, Adam, we find all these meanings interconnected? The three-letter Semitic root (A)DM (םדא) produces all of the following words: *man, mankind, human being, Adam, ground, soil, piece of ground, firmness of earth, be red, red, redness, blood* (Brown et al. 1906: 9–10, 196). This root reflects the idea of (reddish) earth as a source of life, flesh and blood for the existence of man—an ancient concept that is embedded in other cosmogonies from the Middle East as well. The genetic connection between man and earth is also preserved in the language of the Mediterranean cultures—in Latin, the etymology of the word *Homo* (*man, human being, mankind*) is related to *Humus* (*ground, soil*), and both words probably stemmed from the same root in Proto-Indo-European. Therefore, it is possible that the above culturally significant etymology of the word *"man"* in the Semitic language has preserved traces of the most ancient beliefs of mankind, which underlie the eschatological association of red ochre or other red-coloured attributes with life, vital energy and the transformation of inanimate matter into living matter. Thus, the presence of red ochre/hematite, jasper, red object, red textiles, or red colourant in the funeral ritual may be perceived not only as a symbolic allusion, but also as a nonverbal magic formula ensuring the continuation of life in another realm.

Bibliography

Aleshkin VA, Алешкин ВА (1981) "Socialnaja struktura i pogrebalny obrjad kak arheologicheskij istochnik" Социальная структура и погребальны обряд как археологический источник [Social structure and funeral rite like an archaeological source]. Kratkie soobshtenia instituta arheologii Краткие сообщения института археологии [Brief reports of the Institute of Archaeology] 167:3–9

Avramova M, Аврамова М (2008) "Sharenite drehi: po danni ot praistoricheskiya nekropol kam tel Golemiya ostrov, s. Durankulak, Dobrichko" Шарените дрехи: по данни от праисторическия некропол към тел Големия остров, с. Дуранкулак, Добричко [Colorful clothes: according to data from the prehistoric necropolis of the settlement mound on the big island, Durankulak village, Dobrich region]. Po Patya kam minaloto. Sbornik nauchni statii po povod 65-godishninata na d-r Georgi Kitov. По пътя към миналото. Сборник научни статии по повод 65-годишнината на д-р Георги Китов [On the way to the past. Collection of papers on the occasion of the 65th anniversary of Dr. Georgi Kitov]. Sofia, pp 23–29

Bachvarov K, Бъчваров К (2003) Neolitni pogrebalni obredi: Intramuralni grobove ot balgarskite zemi v konteksta na Yugoiztochna Evropa i Anatolia Неолитни погребални обреди: Интрамурални гробове от българските земи в контекста на Югоизточна Европа и Анатолия [Neolithic mortuary practices: intramural burials in Bulgaria in their Southeast European and Anatolian context]. Bard

Bakardzhiev ST, Бакърджиев СТ (2005a) "Spasitelni arheologicheski prouchvania na mogila No. 1 ot mogilen nekropol v m. Golemiya Kayrak pri s. Mogila, obshtina Tundzha" Спасителни археологически проучвания на могила № 1 от могилен некропол в м. Големия Кайряк при с. Могила, Община Тунджа [Rescue archaeological excavations of grave no. 1 from a mound necropolis in the Golemiya Kayryak locality near the village of Mogila, Tundzha municipality]. Arheologicheski otkritiya i razkopki prez 2004 g. XLIV Natsionalna arheologicheska konferentsia. Археологически открития и разкопки през 2004 г. XLIV Национална археологическа конференция [Archaeological discoveries and excavations in 2004. XLIV National archaeological conference]. Sofia, pp 81–82

Bakardzhiev ST, Бакърджиев СТ (2005b) "Spasitelni arheologicheski prouchvania na mogilen nekropol v m. Sabev Bair pri s. Drazhevo, obshtina Tundzha" Спасителни археологически проучвания на могилен некропол в м. Събев Баир при с. Дражево, община Тунджа [Rescue archaeological excavations of a mound necropolis in the Sabev Bair locality near the village of Drazhevo, Tundzha Municipality]. Arheologicheski otkritiya i razkopki prez 2004 g. XLIV Natsionalna arheologicheska konferentsia. Археологически открития и разкопки през 2004 г. XLIV Национална археологическа конференция [Archaeological discoveries and excavations in 2004. XLIV National archaeological conference]. Sofia, pp 150–153

Boyadziev Y (2008) Changes of the burial rites within the transition from Hamangia to Varna culture. Acta Musei Varnaensis VI:85–93

Brown F, Driver S, Briggs C (eds) (1906/2012) A Hebrew and English lexicon of the Old Testament. Oxford

Butzer K (1980) Comments. In: Wreschner E (ed) Red ochre and human evolution: a case for discussion [and comments and reply]. Curr Anthropol 21:635

Chen H (2013) The Qijia culture of the upper yellow river valley. In: Underhill AP (ed) A companion to Chinese archaeology. Wiley-Blackwell, pp 105–124

Clifford A (2012) The geologic model of religion. Andrew Clifford

d'Errico F, Salomon H, Vignaud C, Stringer C (2010) Pigments from the middle palaeolithic levels of Es-Skhul (Mount Carmel, Israel). J Archaeol Sci 37:3099–3110

Derevianko AP, Gao X, Olsen JW, Rybin EP (2012) The paleolithic of Dzungaria (Xinjiang, Northwest China) based on materials from the Luotuoshi site. Archaeol Ethnol Anthropol Eurasia 40(4):2–18

Eliade M, Trask WR (trans) (1978) A history of religious ideas. Volume 1: From the Stone Age to the Eleusinian mysteries. The University of Chicago Press

Gao X (2008) Zhoukoudian upper cave revisited. Curr Anthropol 49(4):732–745

Gao Z 高志伟 (2011) "Kaogu ziliao suojian zheshi, zhusha, qiandan ji qi yingyong" 考古资料所见赭石、朱砂、铅丹及其应用 [Ochre, cinnabar and red lead found in archaeological data and their applications]. Qinghai minzu daxue xuebao 青海民族大学学报. J Qinghai Nationalities Univ 37(1):102–109

Gening V, Borzunov V, Генинг В, Борзунов В (1975) "Metodika statisticheskoij harakteristiki i sravnitelnogo analiza pogrebalnogo obrjada" Методика статистической характеристики и сравнительного анализа погребального обряда [Methods of statistical characteristics and comparative analysis of the funeral rite]. Voprosy arheologii Urala Вопросы археологии Урала. Probl Archaeol Urals 13:42–72

Häusler A (1980) Comments. In: Wreschner E (ed) Red ochre and human evolution: a case for discussion [and comments and reply]. Curr Anthropol 21

Henshilwood CS, d'Errico F, Watts I (2009) Engraved ochres from the middle stone age levels at Blombos Cave, South Africa. J Hum Evol 57(1):27–47

Higham T, Chapman J, Slavchev V, Gaydarska B et al (2008) New AMS radiocarbon dates for the Varna Eneolithic cemetery, Bulgarian Black Sea Coast. Acta Musei Varnaensis VI. Varna, pp 95–114

Izdimirski M Издимирски М (2017) "Tekstil, tsvyat i simvol v trakiyski grobni nahodki ot I hil. pr. Hr." Текстил, цвят и символ в тракийски гробни находки от I хил. пр. Хр. [Textile, colour and symbol in Thracian grave finds from the 1st millennium B.C.]. ΚΡΑΤΙΣΤΟΣ: Sbornik v chest na professor Petar Delev. ΚΡΑΤΙΣΤΟΣ: Сборник в чест на професор Петър Делев [ΚΡΑΤΙΣΤΟΣ: Collection of papers in honor of professor Petar Delev]. Sofia, pp 423–440

Jacobs Z, Duller G, Wintle AG, Henshilwood CS (2006) Extending the chronology of deposits at Blombos cave, South Africa, back to 140 Ka using optical dating of single and multiple gains of quartz. J Human Evol 51(3):255–273

Jones P (2019) Ochre and rust: artefacts and encounters on Australian frontiers. Oxford University Press

Jones A, Macgregor G (eds) (2002) Colouring the past: the significance of colour in archaeological research. Oxford

Knight C, Power C, Watts I (1995) The human symbolic revolution: a Darwinian account. Camb Archaeol J 5(1):74–114

Korenjako V, Кореняко В (1977) Pogrebalnaja obrjadnost kak Sistema (k postanovke problemy Погребальная обрядность как система (к постановке проблемы)" [Funeral rites as a system (to the formulation of the problem)]. Arheologia i voprosy ateizma Археология и вопросы атеизма. Archaeol Probl Atheism 1977:5–7

Kosinskaja L, Ostrushko A, Tonkushina M, Judina E et al Косинская Л, Остроушко А, Тонкушина М, Юдинаидр Е (2016) "Fiziko-himicheskij analiz mineralnyh pigmentov: ohra kak massovy istochnik" Физико-химическийанализминеральныхпигментов: охракак "массовыисточник" [Physicochemical analysis of mineral pigments: Ochre as a "mass source"]. Arheologicheskoe nasledie Urala: ot pervyh otkritii k fundamentalnomu nauchnomu znaniju (XX Uralskoe arheologicheskoe soveshtanie) Археологическое наследие Урала: от первых открытий к фундаментальному научному знанию (XX Уральское археологическое совещание) [Archaeological heritage of the Urals: from the first discoveries to fundamental scientific knowledge (XX Ural archaeological meeting)]. Izhevsk, 376–378

Lenneis E (2007) Mesolithic heritage in early Neolithic burial rituals and personal adornments. Documenta Praehistorica 34:129–137

Li X (2013) The later Neolithic period in the central yellow river valley area, c. 4000–3000 B.C. In: Underhill AP (ed) A companion to Chinese archaeology. Wiley-Blackwell, pp 213–235

Li S 李水城 (2018) "Cong Xinjiang Ayituohan yihao mudi de faxian tan Afannaxiewo wenhua" 从新疆阿依托汗一号墓地的发现谈阿凡纳谢沃文化 [Talking about the Afanasievo culture in relation to the discovery of the Aituohan No. 1 cemetery in Xinjiang]. Xinjiang wenwu 新疆文物. Xinjiang Cultural Relics 1–2:105–121

Li X, Lü E, Zhang Y 李肖, 吕恩国, 张永兵 (2011) "Xinjiang Shanshan Yanghai mudi fajue baogao" 新疆鄯善洋海墓地发掘报告 [Excavations of the Yanghai cemetery in Shanshan (Piquan) County, Xinjiang]. Kaogu xue bao 考古学报. J Archaeol 1:99–166

Liu X 刘学堂 (2008) "Xinjiang diqu shiqian renxing diaoxiang de faxian yu chubu yanjiu" 新疆地区史前人形雕像的发现与初步研究 [The discovery and preliminary research of prehistoric human figures in Xinjiang]. Huaxia kaogu 华夏考古. Chinese Archaeol 3

Liu W 刘武 (2013) "Zaoqi xiandai ren zai Zhongguo de chuxian yu yanbian" 早期现代人在中国的出现与演化 [Emergence and evolution of early modern humans in China]. Renlei xue xuebao 人类学学报. Acta Anthropol Sin 32(3):233–246

Luan F (2013) The Dawenkou culture in the lower yellow river and Huai river basin areas. In: Underhill AP (ed) A companion to Chinese archaeology. Wiley-Blackwell, pp 411–434

Mai H, Yang Y, Abuduresule I, Li W et al (2016) Characterization of cosmetic sticks at Xiaohe cemetery in early bronze age Xinjiang, China. Scien Rep 6. https://www.nature.com/articles/srep18939

Mellaart J (1967) Catalhöyük: a Neolithic town in Anatolia. London

Mellaart J (1975) The Neolithic of the near east. London

Minchev A (2008) Introduction. In: Slavchev V (ed) Acta Musei Varnaensis VI. Varna, pp 7–13

Nicolau AC (2016) El Ocre en la Prehistoria: entre la funcionalidad y el simbolismo [Ochre in prehistory: between functionality and symbolism]. Archivo de Prehistoria Levantina [Levantine Prehistory Arch] XXXI:187–211

Nikolov V, Николов В (2003) Predgovor na nauchnia redaktor Предговор на научния редактор [Foreword by the scientific editor]. In: Bachvarov K (ed) Neolitni pogrebalni obredi: Intramuralni grobove ot balgarskite zemi v konteksta na Yugoiztochna Evropa i Anatolia Неолитни погребални обреди: Интрамурални гробове от българските земи в контекста на Югоизточна Европа и Анатолия [Neolithic mortuary practices: intramural burials in Bulgaria in their Southeast European and Anatolian context]. Bard, pp 9–10

Petrova V (2006) Textile remains from prehistoric graves from the territory of Bulgaria. Izvestiya Na RIM Haskovo Известия На РИМ Хасково [Rep Regional Histor Museum Haskovo] 3:30–34

Petru S (2006) Red, black or white? The dawn of colour symbolism. Documenta Praehistorica XXXIII:203–207

Riel-Salvatore J, Clark GA (2001) Grave markers. Middle and early upper Paleolithic burials and the use of chronotypology in contemporary paleolithic research. Curr Anthropol 42(4):449–478

Rifkin R (2011) Assessing the efficacy of red ochre as a prehistoric hide tanning ingredient. J Afr Archaeol 9(2):131–158

Rifkin R (2012) Processing Ochre in the middle stone age: testing the inference of prehistoric behaviours from actualistically derived experimental data. J Anthropol Arcaeol 31:174–195

Roebroeks W, Sier MJ, Nielsen TK, De Loecker D et al (2012) Use of red ochre by early Neandertals. PNAS 109(6):1889–1894. https://www.pnas.org/content/109/6/1889

Schmandt-Besserat D (1980) Ocher in prehistory: 300,000 years of the use of iron ores as pigments. In: Wertime T, Muhly J (eds) The coming of the age of iron. Yale University Press, New Haven, pp 127–150

Stafford M, Frison G, Stanford D, Ziemans G (2003) Digging for the colour of life: Paleoindian red ochre mining at the powers II site, Platte County, Wyoming, USA. Geoarchaeol: An Int J 18(1):71–90

Stavreva V (2018) Red Ochre—for special dead and dangerous dead (use of red ochre in the burial practices during the late Eneolithic by data from the territory of Bulgaria. Pontica 51:115–133

Sun H (2013) The Sanxingdui culture of the Sichuan basin. In: Underhill AP (ed) A companion to Chinese archaeology. Wiley-Blackwell, pp 147–168

Tian L 田露梅 (2018) Zhongguo gudai hongse yanliao kao (shuoshi xuewei lunwen) 中国古代红色颜料考 (硕士学位论文) [Research on red pigments in ancient china (Master's Thesis)]. Available at: http://cdmd.cnki.com.cn/Article/CDMD-10718-1018230199.htm

Todorova H (2003) Prehistory of Bulgaria. In: Recent research in the prehistory of the Balkans, pp 257–328

Velo J (1984) Ochre as medicine: a suggestion for interpretation of the archaeological record. Curr Anthropol 25(5):674

Wadley L (2005) Putting Ochre to the test: replication studies of adhesives that may have been used for hafting tools in the middle stone age. J Hum Evol 49:587–601

Wang Y, Hou H, Yan X, Xia L, Tian X, Zhang J, Ai T, Hu X, Yu J 王永强, 侯知军, 闫雪梅, 夏立栋, 田小红, 张杰, 艾涛, 胡兴军, 于建军 (2018) "2017 nian Xinjiang kaogu shouhuo" 2017 年新疆考古收获 [Results from archaeological research in Xinjiang in 2017]. Xiyu yanjiu 西域研究. Western Region Stud 3:126–136

Wreschner EE, Bolton R, Butzer K, Delporte H et al (1980) Red Ochre and human evolution: a case for discussion [and comments and reply]. Curr Anthropol 21(5):631–644

Wu X 吴新智 (1961) "Zhoukoudian Shandingdong ren huashi de yanjiu" 周口店山顶洞人化石的研究 [Research on human fossils from the upper cave in Zhoukoudian]. Gu jizhui dongwu yu gu renlei 古脊椎动物与古人类. Vertebr Paleontol Paleoanthropol 3(3):181–203

Xinjiang Wenwu Kaogu Yanjiu Suo (2004) 新疆文物考古研究所 [Institute of cultural relics and archaeology of Xinjiang]. "2002 nian Xiaohe mudi kaogu diaocha yu fajue baogao" 2002 年小河墓地考古调查与发掘报告 [2002 Excavation report of Xiaohe cemetery]. Bianjiang kaogu yanjiu 边疆考古研究. Front Archaeol Res 00:338–411

Xu H (2013) The Erlitou culture. In: Underhill AP (ed) A companion to Chinese archaeology. Wiley-Blackwell, pp 300–322

Yu J 于建军 (2018) "2016–2017 nian Xinjiang Jimunai xian Tongtian dong yizhi kaogu fajue xin faxian" 2016–2017 年新疆吉木乃县通天洞遗址考古发掘新发现 [New discovery from archaeological excavations at Tongtiandong site in Jimunai County, Xinjiang]. Xiyu yanjiu 西域研究. Western Regions Stud 1:132–135

Yuan G (2013) The discovery and study of the early Shang culture. In: Underhill AP (ed) A companion to Chinese archaeology. Wiley-Blackwell, pp 323–342

Zanotti DG (1984/1985) Varna: the Necropolis and the gold finds. Talanta 16/17:53–73

Zhao C (2013) The Longshan culture in central Henan province, c. 2600–1900 B.C. In: Underhill AP (ed) A companion to Chinese archaeology. Wiley-Blackwell, pp 236–254

Chapter 4
An Archaeological Study of Early Nomadic Cultural Settlements in the Eastern Tianshan Mountain Region

Jianxin Wang and Lin Xi

Abstract One of the basic characteristics of the nomadic northland is that settlement life was a subordinate concomitant of the main nomadic lifestyle. Therefore, settlement sites exist commonly in that region. Through extensive survey and small-scale excavation in the broad steppes of northwest Gansu and northern Xinjiang in 2000 to 2007, archaeologists have revealed on the whole the distribution law of the ancient nomadic culture's settlements in the steppes of Northwest China. It has been known that these settlements usually leftover dwelling vestiges, tombs, rock paintings and some other basic elements of settlements in the ancient nomadic culture. A comprehensive study provides preliminary know ledge on the cultural features of and interrelation between the two types of early nomadic cultural remains that were distributed in the eastern Tianshan Mountain region.

Keywords Eastern Tianshan Mountain region · Early nomadic culture · Settlement archaeology · Western Han period · Xiongnu

I

Did ancient nomads have a "permanent" residence? Did ancient nomadic cultures leave settlement remains? This has not been clearly understood in our historical and archaeological academia for a long time.

Since ancient nomads, especially early ones, left little documentation of their own history, our study of the history of ancient nomads in northern China can only be based on Chinese texts, which is the same as European scholars have relied on ancient Greek, Roman and Persian texts. However, most of the authors of those texts lived in sedentary areas and lacked first-hand experience of nomadic life, resulting in a somewhat one-sided account of nomadic life. The same lack of understanding

J. Wang (✉)
School of Cultural Heritage, Northwest University, Xi'an, China
e-mail: 13319185059@163.com

L. Xi
Shaanxi Academy of Archaeology, Xi'an, China

© SDX Joint Publishing 2023
X. Li (ed.), *Major Archaeological Discoveries Along the Chinese Silk Road*, Silk Road Research Series, https://doi.org/10.1007/978-981-99-0659-8_5

of nomadic life has led many future generations of scholars to interpret the accounts of ancient texts in a further biased manner.

For example, Sima Qian, in *Biographies of the Xiongnu in Historical Records*, argued that "the Xiongnu move with their livestock to the area with water and grass, not live a life with the cultivation in their cities and towns"[1]; According to Du You in *Tong Dian-Bianfang* chapter: "they live with the water and grass …… and move out when the grass is gone, living without a fixed place".[2] The influence of these ancient authoritative accounts was so profound that many historians and archaeologists have been influenced by them until modern times. As a result, it seems to have been a long-standing tendency for scholars to assume that ancient nomads did not have permanent dwellings and that it was difficult to find traces of their dwellings and even to find a site. This understanding has had a direct impact on archaeological practice, with the result that archaeological research on ancient nomadic cultures in the grasslands of northern China has so far consisted mainly of burial material, with little research on settlements, in contrast to the large number of archaeological discoveries and research on settlements in the sedentary agricultural regions, centred on the Yellow River basin and the Yangtze River valley.

Although the climate of the northern China has fluctuated somewhat over the past 3000 years in response to global climate change, the long and cold winters of the steppe area have not changed significantly over the millennia due to the high latitude and altitude of this region. Under these climatic conditions, it is impossible for pastoralists to live a nomadic life in the freezing winter, and they must find sheltered, sunny, water and grass-rich places in order to survive the winter. Therefore, the existence of nomadic winter camps in the northern steppe areas of Eurasia is beyond doubt. Some foreign scholars have noted the existence of nomadic cultural settlements.[3] We have found that nomadism with settlement has been the basic way of life for nomads in the northern steppe from ancient times to the present.

However, the winter camps were not only used in winter. When summer arrives and the herders go out on the grasslands, the old, the sick, women and children who are unable to cope with the upheaval of life do not necessarily follow the young and the strong to herd their animals, but often stay in the winter camps. The winter camps are therefore in use virtually all year round. Pregnant women are generally expected to stay in the winter camps, and so the majority of herders are born in the winter camps. Thus, in this sense, the winter camps are their true home. In this way, if they had a relatively stable place to live, they must have left behind the remains of that place. Thus, sites of ancient nomadic settlements are common in the steppe area of northern China.

---

[1] *Historical Records—The Chronicles of Xiongnu*.

[2] Under the entry of "Border Defense XVI" in the "*General Dictionary—Border Defense Code*".

[3] a. János Hamatta, Nomadic and Sedentary life in the Great Steppes Belt of Eurasia, The Archaeology of the Steppes: Methods and Strategies, Papers from the *International Symposium held in Naples 9–12 November 1992*, pp. 565–573, edited by Bruno Genito, Napoli, 1994.

b. István Erdélyi, The Settlements of Hsiung-nu, The Archaeology of the Steppes: Methods and Strategies, Papers from the *International Symposium held in Naples 9–12 November 1992*, pp. 553–565, edited by Bruno Genito, Napoli, 1994.

Where to find the sites of ancient nomadic settlements? Because the steppe area was the environment in which nomads lived, it is tempting to think that it is this place that the sites of ancient nomadic settlements should be located. It should be noted, however, that nomadic life on the grasslands was mainly during the summer. In the course of their constant migration, the short duration of a settlement and the form of housing used, such as yurt and tents, made it difficult to leave many deposits and visible remains. In addition, the open grassland is susceptible to wind erosion, and even if there is some accumulation, it will easily disappear. As a result, it is difficult to find nomadic settlement sites on the grasslands, except for a few special relics. In winter, herders had to find shelter with sun, water and grass from the wind, and only mountains and hills could provide such environmental conditions. The winter camps of ancient nomads were therefore generally located on the south or south-east side of the mountains and hills.

Due to the constraints of topography and resources, especially water resources, most winter camps can only meet the survival needs of a small number of herders and livestock. Therefore, the winter camps with nomadic families should be abundant in a small scale. Since 2000, we have conducted an extensive survey in the Eastern Tianshan region from north-western Gansu to north-eastern Xinjiang. More than 200 sites of ancient nomadic cultures have been investigated and discovered, most of which are small-scale settlements. Most of these settlements are located on the south or south-east side of mountains and hills, and often coincide with modern herders' winter camps, which has become one of the patterns of distribution of ancient nomadic sites we found during our survey.

The ancient and modern choice of winter camps by nomads combined with the limited number of sites with such conditions means that there is a very high probability that the settlement sites of modern nomadic cultures overlap with the locations of ancient winter camps. This distribution pattern also suggests that the ancient sites that largely coincide with the locations of modern nomadic winter camps should be the remains of ancient nomads.

In winter, both ordinary herding families and nobles and rulers had to settle. Therefore, the winter settlement sites of ancient nomadic cultures distributed on the south or south-east side of mountains and hills have a large number of small sites as well as a small number of medium and large sites. Small sites, medium and large sites of the same period and culture are often closely linked in terms of geographical distribution.

In the summer, the ordinary nomadic families lived a nomadic life on the grasslands with water and grass, without a place to settle, so it is difficult to find small sites of ancient nomadic culture in the summer pastures. Large and medium-sized sites are different from small ones; they not only had winter camps, but also distributed in the summer pasture. This is because the ancient nomadic clan nobles, tribal leaders and higher rulers had to move with the majority of herders for the convenience of their rule and for security reasons. They moved to the summer pastures with the majority of herdsmen in summer, but they did not go to the grasslands with the common herdsmen to graze their livestock, rather they would find a suitable place to settle near the summer pastures and establish a summer ruling centre at all levels.

Therefore, the large and medium-sized settlement sites of ancient nomads often have a winter and summer division. Even the king's court, which was the highest ruling centre of ancient nomads, had both winter and summer courts.

For a summer camp of ancient nomadic culture, the location of large and medium-sized settlements often selected in the summer pasture near the northern slope of the mountain range as it is a high and open terrain with abundant water with an easy access. This is not only convenient for living, but also easy to observe the situation of herdsmen grazing on the grasslands, to timely detect the emergencies and take measures. Moreover, it is a reflection of the ruler's supreme power.

II

In the southern and south-eastern side of Eastern Tianshan region, it is the present-day Hami City, Xinjiang[4] and the Mazongshan region in north-western Gansu,[5] there are a large number of ancient nomadic culture of winter settlements, including a large number of small settlement sites, and a small number of large and medium-sized settlement sites. The grasslands at the northern foot of the Eastern Tianshan from Yiwu to Balikun, especially the Balikun Basin which has a large grassland area, have been rich in water and grass since ancient times, with cool climate and abundant rainfall in summer, and are the traditional summer pastures of nomads. There are some small settlement sites as winter camps at the southern foot of Moqinwula Mountain on the northern edge of the Balikun Basin, while the settlement sites of ancient nomadic culture found in some water-rich and open topographic gully areas on the northern slope of the Eastern Tianshan at the southern edge of the Basin[6] are all large and medium-sized settlements, where the small sites are basically missing. The altitude of Balikun and Yiwu is relatively high, generally reaching about 2000 m, so the winter is cold and long, with the lowest temperature reaching minus − 30–40 °C. Therefore, the northern slope of the Eastern Tianshan is only suitable for summer residence, and the large and medium-sized settlement sites of ancient nomadic culture distributed here are probably the ruling centres of ancient nomads at all levels in the summer near the grazing land.

Since it is a place of residence, there should be the remains of occupation. The dwelling sites of ancient nomadic cultures found in the Eastern Tianshan area are generally distributed with stone enclosed, mostly square or rectangular in plan, as well as round.[7] Since the ancient and modern nomads living in the Eastern Tianshan area have been commonly using stone to build dwelling places, burial sites, animal

---

[4] "Hami Cultural Relics" compilation group: *"Hami Cultural Relics"*, Xinjiang People's Publishing House, 1993.

[5] Cultural Heritage and Archaeology Research Center of Northwestern University, Gansu Institute of Cultural Relics and Archaeology, Gansu Province: "Briefing on Archaeological Investigations in the Mazong Mountains of Gansu", *Archaeology and Cultural Relics*, No. 5, 2006.

[6] "Hami Cultural Relics" compilation group: *"Hami Cultural Relics"*, Xinjiang People's Publishing House, 1993.

[7] a. Archaeology Department of Northwestern University, Cultural Management Committee of Hami Prefecture: "Survey of the Site Group of Xinjiang Balikun Yegongtai a Xiheigou", *Archaeology and Cultural Relics,* No. 2, 2005.

fences and enclosed pasture, there have been different perceptions of these dwelling sites in the past, with some researchers considering them to be burial, and many others even not recognizing them as ancient sites.

In the course of our investigation, we found that a few ancient remains, such as pottery sherds, were often scattered in some of the stone enclosure dwelling sites. In addition, from 2006 to 2007, we excavated four stone-walled dwelling sites in Dongheigou (also known as Shirenzigou), Balikun County, and found ancient occupational remains, including pillar holes, fire pits and other remains, as well as pottery, lithic, bone artefacts, bronze and iron objects,[8] indicating that these remains should be the dwelling site of ancient nomadic people. Based on the archaeological data available so far, it is difficult to confirm whether the superstructure of these dwelling remains is a wooden structure or a tent. Both wooden structures and tents are organic materials, which no longer exist. However, judging from the thin, few and sparse distribution of the holes of the load-bearing columns in the excavated sites, it is more likely that the superstructure of these dwelling sites was a lighter weight tent.

Although the forms of the discovered living remains do not vary much, they can still be one of the bases for distinguishing and confirming the archaeological culture of ancient nomadic people. There are square and round shapes, indicating that they belong to different times and cultures. Among the modern nomads in China, the yurt of Mongolians and Kazakhs are round in plan, while the tents of Tibetans are square and rectangular in plan. Therefore, different forms of dwelling relics might also be related to different nomadic peoples.

The tombs of ancient nomadic cultures in the Eastern Tianshan area are in various forms. Judging from the plan view, there are round, square and rectangular ones; from the sealing pile, there are the tombs without sealing pile, or with stone sealing pile, earth pile, and mixed earth-stone sealing pile; there are also differences between round and square sealing piles; from the surface facilities around the burial, there are some tombs without stone fence, some has round stone fence or square stone fence, or beard-like and radial ones, and there are stone figures and altars in front of some burial. In addition, there are different types of building stones, such as pebble, rock, slate and so on. These differences of burial reflect the burial customs of various ethnic groups.

Petroglyphs and rock painting are also important remains related to ancient nomadic culture. Petroglyphs are widely distributed in the steppe areas of northern Eurasia from the Great and Small Xinganling Mountains in the east to the Black Sea and Caspian Sea in the west. The petroglyphs mostly reflect nomadic life. In our investigation, we found that there are often sites of nomadic culture near the

---

b. Cultural Heritage and Archaeology Research Center of Northwestern University, Cultural Relics Bureau of Hami Prefecture, Cultural Management Committee of Balikun County: "Survey of the Site of Xinjiang Balikun Dongheigou", *Archaeology and Cultural Relics*, No. 5, 2006.

[8] Xinjiang Institute of Cultural Relics and Archaeology, Center for Cultural Heritage and Archaeology, Northwestern University: "2006 Excavations at the Dongheigou Site in Balikun, Xinjiang", *Xinjiang Cultural Relics*, No. 2, 2007.

petroglyph sites which is an important rule. In this way, the petroglyphs can be a guide to find nomadic culture sites.

At present, petroglyph researchers in China are mainly artists and ethnologists, and archaeologists are rarely involved. The published works on petroglyphs mainly interpret the content of petroglyphs. Most of the investigations and records of petroglyphs have not paid attention to the coexistence between these petroglyphs, and the surrounding ancient dwelling ruins and burials, and there is a lack of comprehensive research on their relationship; at the same time, the records of petroglyphs are generally inaccurate and not objective. Since petroglyphs are basically carved on natural rocks, issues such as the date of petroglyphs, cultural attributes and the identity of authors have been a bottleneck for petroglyph research.

In our investigation, we found that the petroglyphs on the same rock or even on the same surface of the rock were not necessarily carved at the same time. Many researchers often do not carefully identify and distinguish these cases, and then interpret the petroglyphs on the same surface or even on the same rock as the one picture, which is inevitably a mistake. Since petroglyphs are an important part of the remains of ancient nomadic culture that coexisted with settlement remains and burials, archaeologists cannot abandon their responsibility and must participate in the investigation and study of petroglyphs.

First of all, the record of petroglyphs must be as objective and accurate as possible. The development of modern science and technology has made such a record possible. The record itself is one of the means to protect the rock paintings, because many of them will disappear soon due to anthropogenic and natural damage.

How to conduct the study of petroglyph? We have been exploring in practice and have gradually developed a method to study petroglyphs using archaeological stratigraphy and archaeological typology.[9] Due to the differences in carving tools, techniques and cultural traditions, there are obvious distinctions in the expression of petroglyphs from various periods and cultures. Petroglyphs carved with stone tools are coarse and broad in expression with thick lines or just an outline, whereas those carved with metal tools are delicate in expression with thin lines. It is noteworthy that there are petroglyphs of different forms on many rocks, and there is often a superimposed or breaking relationship between different forms of petroglyphs on the same rocks. Based on these characteristics, it is not only necessary but also possible to apply the methods of archaeological typology and stratigraphy to the study of petroglyphs.

In our research practice, we have recorded and studied different forms of petroglyphs on the rocks in terms of their superimposed breakage, spatial location, and the colour of the petroglyphs, i.e. the degree of weathering determined by the early and late carving time of the petroglyphs. Accurate partitioning of petroglyphs is the basis of petroglyph recording and research. The same petroglyph refers to those carved

---

[9] a. Cultural Heritage and Archaeology Research Center of Northwestern University and Xinjiang Institute of Cultural Relics and Archaeology: "Investigation of Qiongkeke Rock Paintings in Nileke, Xinjiang", *Archaeology and Cultural Relics*, No. 5, 2006.

b. Wang Jianxin and He Junfeng: "Study on the Classification and Staging of Qiongkeke Rock Paintings", *Archaeology and Cultural Relics*, No. 5, 2006.

at roughly the same time, and should have generally the same expression, similar colours and carving techniques, a relatively concentrated distribution in spatial location, and a related picture content. A single image, such as a specific animal, figure or object, is the smallest unit for rock art recording and study.

A single image can be equivalent to a single relic; a kind of petroglyphs can be equivalent to a class of relics; a single petroglyph can be equivalent to a relic unit; multiple petroglyphs on a rock can be equivalent to multiple relic units with a sequential order. Multiple petroglyphs on different rocks at one site can be grouped according to the expression of petroglyphs, and then the relative chronological relationship between the groups can be confirmed according to the stratigraphic relationship.

Different forms of rock art should be related to the cultures and peoples in different times. Similarly, different forms of tombs and dwelling sites should be related to the cultures of different eras and ethnic groups. Since petroglyphs exist in the same site with dwelling remains and burials, there must be some coexistence between petroglyphs and a certain type of dwelling remains and burials. We can first study the relative chronology of rock paintings, dwelling remains and burials separately, and then gradually confirm the coexisting relationship between them.

It is not possible to confirm this concurrent relationship by studying only one site, so we must study several sites in a certain area and verify them repeatedly before we can finally confirm them. Of course, we can start with the sites where discovered relatively simple forms of rock paintings, dwelling remains and burials, and then study those sites with complex cultural factors of rock paintings, dwelling remains and burials of different eras and cultures.

Dwelling remains, burials and petroglyphs are the basic elements of ancient nomadic cultural sites, and we must insist on a comprehensive study of these three types of remains in order to reveal the cultural landscape of ancient nomads in a more comprehensive manner. With regard to the problem of dating and cultural attributes of rock art, as long as we effectively apply the methods of archaeological typology and stratigraphy and the integrated study of the three types of remains, it is possible to solve the problem after a period of time.

The study of settlement remains and burial is also an important part of the archaeological research of ancient nomadic culture settlements. However, it should be noted that because of the distinctions in production and lifestyle between ancient nomadic and sedentary peoples and their living environment, the objects and methods of study of relics should be different. In the areas where agricultural cultures were distributed, pottery became the main object of archaeological research and an important basis for distinguishing and confirming archaeological cultures which is because pottery is a widely used and commonly made object in agricultural areas. In the area where nomadic culture was distributed, although pottery was also used, it was fragile and not easy to carry during moving, so it is impossible to use it in large quantities. In the life of herdsmen, metal, wood and leather are the objects that are used in large quantities. At the same time, in the northern steppe areas where nomadic culture is distributed, it is also impossible to make pottery in general. Because most of the terrain in these areas is subject to constant wind erosion, it is difficult to form soil accumulation, so as a raw material for pottery production of clay accumulation is limited.

Among the pottery excavated from ancient nomadic culture sites found in the Eastern Tianshan area, three phenomena are noteworthy. First, the number of the pottery found is relatively small; second, the types and forms of pottery discovered at the same site are diverse and unrelated, making it difficult to conduct archaeological typological research; third, some of the same forms of pottery are found in a wide area that includes both agricultural and nomadic areas. We believe that all three phenomena are related to the production and lifestyle of nomadic peoples. The first phenomenon suggests that nomads used pottery in smaller quantities, the second indicates that nomads used pottery from a variety of sources, and the third is likely because nomads brought pottery from the same location to different regions. Some researchers have failed to pay sufficient attention to these phenomena, and have simply applied the way of thinking and research methods used in the study of pottery from agricultural cultures to the study of nomadic cultures, and even made conclusions about the characteristics and distribution range of archaeological cultures in grassland areas based only on the discovery and distribution of pottery. The persuasion of such conclusions is obviously doubtful.

Nevertheless, the study of pottery is still an important element in the study of ancient nomadic cultural relics. In addition to the archaeological typology of pottery, the study of the provenance and process of circulation of pottery should be the centre to identify the actual use and production of pottery in nomadic culture. Only in this way can the role and significance of pottery research in the study of the remains of ancient nomadic cultures be truly clarified.

Metal weapons, tools, harnesses and ornaments are commonly found in the ancient nomadic cultural relics in the northern steppe areas of Eurasia and have become important objects of archaeological research on nomadic culture. Due to the activity of nomadic people and the widely distribution of their activities, the metal tools in the remains of nomadic culture have similarity and connection in a wide range of areas, but at the same time, we should also see that the metal tools of different ethnic groups and cultures differ to a certain extent in form or ornamentation, which requires us to observe and study the form and ornamentation of metal tools more carefully. For example, animal motifs are commonly found in the remains of ancient nomadic cultures in the northern steppe region of Eurasia. Some scholars have regarded these animal motifs as a feature of ancient Scythian culture, and thus the cultures that used them are regarded as ancient Scythian culture. In recent years, archaeologists from different countries have found that the forms and ornaments of animal decorations from different regions and cultures have different characteristics, and they should belong to different peoples.[10]

---

[10] Natal'ja L. Clenova, On the Degree of Similarity between Material Culture Components within the Scythian World', The Archaeology of the Steppes: Methods and Strategies, Papers from the *International Symposium held in Naples 9–12 November 1992*, pp. 499–540, edited by Bruno Genito, Napoli, 1994.

In addition to artefacts, architectural relics are also important for archaeological research on ancient nomadic cultures. In contrast to the architectural traditions of the Yellow River Basin and the Yangtze River Basin, which were centred on the agricultural culture, the settlement sites of ancient nomadic cultures distributed along the mountains are generally popular with stone structured dwelling ruins and burials, and petroglyphs are carved on natural rocks. Moreover, in the northern steppe areas, the weathering is so common that there is less late-period accumulation, and many remains can be found on the surface. Therefore, in addition to the necessary archaeological excavation of the settlement remains and burials to understand their lower structure, cultural attributes and chronology, surface survey can be the main way of work for the study of ancient nomadic cultural relics.

The investigation and study of ancient nomadic cultural relics can help us to understand the distribution of different forms of relics and the cultures they represent, as well as the distribution of various types of cultural remains of the same period within the same site. Such research is not only of great academic significance in the field of archaeological research on ancient nomadic culture, but also an important basis for research on the conservation of nomadic cultural sites, including site conservation planning. In the process of archaeological investigation and excavation of the Dongheigou site, we have tried the way of synchronizing the research work of site conservation planning with archaeological work which turns out a good result.

III

After 8 years of archaeological fieldwork, we have made significant achievements in the archaeological research of early nomadic culture settlements in the Eastern Tianshan area and have basically mastered the distribution pattern of ancient nomadic culture settlement sites and discovered a large number of settlement sites. Among them, there are five large settlement sites of early nomadic culture found in the north and south sides of East Tianshan. These five sites are the Yuegongtai-Xiheigou site group, Dongheigou site and Hongshankou site in the territory of Balikun County at the northern foot of the Eastern Tianshan Mountains, and the Wulatai site and Xishan site in the territory of Hami City at the southern foot of the Eastern Tianshan Mountains.

Today's Eastern Tianshan is known in Han dynasty literature as "Qilian Mountain", "Qilian Tianshan Mountain" or "Tianshan Mountain". "Qilian" is the phonetic name, "Tianshan" is the name of the translation, and "Qilian Tianshan" is the name of the phonetic name with the translation, both should be the nomenclature of Han Dynasty on the Eastern Tianshan Mountain. On this point, the famous scholar Yan Shigu in the Tang Dynasty for the *"Book of Han· The Chronicle of Emperor Wu"* and the *"Book of Han· The Chronicle of Huo Qubing"*, and *"Book of Han· The Chronicle of Zhangqian"* clearly stated in the commentary, and it is also evidenced by the records of the *Historical Records* and the *Book of Han* itself.[11]

---

[11] Wang Jianxin, "New Progress in the Study of Ancient Nomadic Culture in the Grasslands of Northwest China: An Archaeological Exploration of the Ancient Yuezhi Culture," in *Zhou, Qin, Han, and Tang Studies (3rd Series)*, pp. 240–241, Sanqin Publishing House, 2004.

Before the second century B.C., the centre of activity of the ancient Yuezhi and Wusun peoples should be in the area of the Eastern Tianshan Mountain, their winter camps should be at southern foothill, their summer pastures should be on north side, and there should be winter and summer royal courts on the both sides of the Eastern Tianshan Mountain, which is also consistent with the documentary record that they all lived in "between Dunhuang and Qilian Mountain."[12] Before 161 B.C., during the reign of the old Xiongnu Shangchanyu, the Xiongnu finally defeated the Yuezhi, and most of the Yuezhi, the Great Yuezhi, were forced to move westward, after which the Xiongnu occupied their land.[13] From the time of Emperor Wu of Han Dynasty, the Western Han Dynasty sent troops to the Eastern Tianshan area to fight against the Xiongnu in order to counter the Xiongnu. The following examples are recorded in the literature.

1. In the *"Record of History"*, the chapter of *"Biography of Xiongnu"*, *"Biography of General Wei"* and *"Biography of Dayuan"*, and the *"Biography of Huo Qubing"* and *"Biography of Zhang Qian"* in the *"Book of Han"*, it is recorded that in the summer of the second year of Emperor Wu's Yuanshou (121 B.C.), General Huo Qubing led an army to attack the Xiongnu in the eastern Tianshan region.

In the *Historical Records· the Xiongnu Biography*, it records: "in (the second year of Yuanshou) summer, there are tens of thousands of cavalries out of Longxi to the north of the two thousand miles to attack the Xiongnu. After passing through Juyan, attacking Qilian Mountain, they got more than 30,000 captives, more than 70 people are nobles". In *Historical Records· General Wei's biography* also recorded Emperor Wu's comments on this battle: "General overcame Juyan, then crossed the small yuezhi, attacked Qilian Mountain, and got the head of King Tu of the chiefdom …", indicating that the king's court of the Xiongnu must have been in the area of the Eastern Tianshan Mountain. *Historical Records· Biography of Dayuan* records "in the next year (of the second year of Yuanshou), Qian was promoted as Lieutenant, and he attacked the Xiongnu to the north with General Li. Xiongnu surrounded General Li, the army suffered heavy losses, and Qian should be beheaded but he was redeemed

---

[12] a. *"Historical Records· The chronicle of Dayuan"* records: "the first Yuezhi live in between Dunhuang and Qilian".
b. *"The book of Han· The chronicle of the Western Region· The Great Yuezhi"* records: "The Great Yuezhi originally lived between Dunhuang and Qilian".

[13] a. *"Historical Records The chronicle of Dayuan"* record: "the great Yuezhi is to the west of Dayuan, living in the north of the Gui River. It is located at the south of the Daxia (大夏), west of the Anxi (安息), and north of the Kangju (康居). This is a moving state, with the herds migration, shares the same customs with Xiongnu. The population could be one or two hundred thousand. Therefore, when the state is strong, they can easily defeat Xiongnu. However, when Modu (冒顿) monarch established, he led army attacked the Yuezhi and killed the king and made his head as a drinking vessel.
b. *The Book of Han· The chronicle of West Region*, the entry of "great Yuezhi": "great Yuezhi is a moving state, migrating with the herds and sharing the similar custom with Xiongnu. When they are strong, they had a population more than 100,000, so, they disdained Xiongnu. Originally, they lived in between Dunhuang and Qilian. Afterwards, monarch Modu attacked the Yuezhi, and the monarch Laoshang (老上) killed the king of Yuezhi, with its head as a drinking vessel. As a consequence, Yuezhi moved far away".

as a commoner. At the same year, Han sent another General to break Xiongnu west area and conquered tens of thousands of soldiers to Qilian Mountain. In the next year, the king of Hunxie led their people surrendered to Han, and there were no Xiongnu between Jincheng, Hexi and South Mountain to Yanze anymore". *The Book of Han· Zhang Qian's biography* also has the same account.[14] Obviously, here the "South Mountain" is the present Qilian Mountain, and the "Qilian Mountain" and the "South Mountain" show up in this account at the same time, which suggests that the Han dynasty's record of the Qilian Mountain is not the present Qilian Mountain.

Slightly later than the *"Historical Record"*, the document *"Salt and Iron Record—Criticism on Qin Dynasty"* recorded: "So the former emperor mobilized soldiers to conquer the Xiongnu, and then broke Qilian Tianshan Mountain …… Hunxie led his people to surrender". It is also important circumstantial evidence that the Qilian Mountains, the destination of this battle, is the Eastern Tianshan and not the present Qilian Mountains.

2. The *Chronicle of Xiongnu* and the *Chronicle of General Li* in the *Historical Records* and the *Chronicle of Emperor Wu* and the *Chronicle of Xiongnu* in the *Book of Han* all record that in the second year of the Tianhan (99 B.C.), General Li Guangli led the army to attack the Xiongnu's noble to the Eastern Tianshan Mountains.

The *Historical Records· The Chronicle of General Li* records: "the second year of Tianhan autumn,[15] General Li Guangli led 30,000 cavalries to attack Xiongnu noble at Qilian Tianshan". *Historical Records·The Chronicle of Xiongnu* records: "next year (the second year of Tianhan), Han sent General Guangli with 30,000 cavalries out of Jiuquan (酒泉). The noble was attacked in Tianshan and Li returned with more than 10,000 captives." This is slightly different from the record in the *Historical Records of General Li*, in that it changes "Qilian Tianshan" to "Tianshan" and explicitly refers to its location as "out of Jiuquan", indicating that the destination of Li Guangli's campaign was the eastern part of Qilian Tianshan rather than the present Qilian Mountain. *The Book of Han's Chronicle of Emperor Wu* and *the Chronicle of Xiongnu* give roughly the same account of this event as the *Chronicle of Xiongnu in Historical Records*. These accounts also provide us with the important information that the king's court of the Xiongnu noble was probably located in the area of the Eastern Tianshan Mountains.

3. *The Book of Han· the Chronicle of Xiongnu, the Chronicle of Emperor Xuan* and the *Chronicle of the Western Regions* all record that in the second (72 B.C.) and third (71 B.C.) years of Emperor Xuan's Ben Shi, the Han army united with Wusun to attack on the right part of Xiongnu to the East Tianshan area.

---

[14] *The Book of Han· Biography of Zhangqian*: "this year (the second year of the Yuanshou), the general of Han broke the Xiongnu western side, killing tens of thousands of people, to Qilian Mountain. In the autumn, King Hunxie (浑邪王) surrendered to Han, and there is no Xiongnu in the areas of Jincheng, Hexi and Nanshan to Yanze".

[15] *The Book of Han* records the time of this battle as "May in Summer".

The Book of Han· the Chronicle of Xiongnu record: "the second year of Benshi, the Han court sent Guandong light cavalry who were selected as they are healthy people and good at riding and shooting. Tian Guangming was assigned as Qilian general with more than 40,000 cavalries out of the West River; the general an Mingyou led more than 30,000 soldiers out of Zhangye; the front general Han Zeng commanded more than 30,000 cavalries out of Yunzhong; the general Zhao Chongguo has more than 30,000 soldiers out of Jiuquan; Yunzhong governor Tian Shun also led more than 30,000 soldiers out of Wuyuan: all five generals, with more than 100,000 soldiers, attacked into steppe area more than 1000 kms each. And the lieutenant Chang Hui sent troops to the western region of Wusun, with a following 50,000 cavalries from the west. So, together with the five generals of the army, there are more than 200,000 people. Xiongnu heard that the Han army out of the plains, the old and weak ran away and drove the herds far away, so as to reduce the five generals gain". "General Zhao Chongguo and his army should combine with Wusun attacked Xiongnu at Puleize, but Wusun first arrived, and the Han army did not catch up with the former ... Lieutenant Chang Hui and Wusun soldiers attacked the right valley Li court and captured the lord's father line and a thousand chiefs, the following general more than 39,000 people. They also seized horses, cattle, sheep, donkeys, mules, camels more than 700,000." In the *Book of the Han*, the chapter of *Chronicle of Emperor Xuan* and the *Biography of the Western Regions* also have more or less the same record on this matter.[16] The Han Dynasty's Puleize is the present-day Balikun Lake,[17] which indicates that the king's Li court of the Xiongnu was located in the area of the present-day Balikun Steppe at the northern foot of the Eastern Tianshan Mountains.

It is worth noting that the above mentioned three battles between the Han army and Xiongnu in the Eastern Tianshan area during the Western Han period were all in summer, which means that the royal courts of Xiongnu attacked by Huo Qubing, Li Guangli, and Chang Hui and Wusun soldiers should all be summer royal courts, which should be distributed in the area of Balikun and Yiwu at the northern foot of the Eastern Tianshan.

From the documented history of the Xiongnu, the right line of the Xiongnu, which occupied the homeland of the Yuezhi during the Western Han dynasty, differed from the Yuezhi in that they only went to the grasslands of Balikun and Yiwu at the northern foot of the Eastern Tianshan Mountains to graze their livestock in summer, and returned to their winter camps on the Mongolian plateau to settle in winter.

After the Xiongnu internal conflicts in the late Western Han Dynasty, the split of Xiongnu between the north and the south during the Eastern Han Dynasty, the defection of the southern Xiongnu to the Han Dynasty, and the rise of the Xianbei and other ethnic groups, the area of the Northern Xiongnu activities in the Eastern Han Dynasty gradually moved westward, and the Eastern Tianshan area became

---

[16] a. *The Book of Han. The Chronicle of Emperor Xuan.*
  b. *The Book of Han. Biography of the Western Regions.*

[17] Cen Zhongmian: "*The Geography of the Western Region in the Book of Han (2nd volume)*", China Book Bureau, 1981. In this book, pp. 446–456, Pulei, Puleize, and Puleihou country are examined and interpreted.

the central area of the Northern Xiongnu. According to the *Book of East Han* and other documents and the Eastern Han inscriptions, the Han army fought against the Northern Xiongnu in the Eastern Tianshan area for many times during the Eastern Han period.

1. In 73 AD, in the 16th year of Yongping, Emperor Ming of the Han Dynasty, Lieutenant Dou Gu and Lieutenant Geng Zhong led an army to attack the Northern Xiongnu to the Eastern Tianshan area.

   The *Book of Later Han · Dou Rong's Biography* records: "(Dou) Ku and Geng Zhong reached Tianshan and attacked King Huyan beheading more than a thousand heads. King Huyan escaped and was chased to Pulei sea. They left the officials and soldiers in Yiwulu city". It means that the kingdom of King Huyan of the Northern Xiongnu was in the area of the Eastern Tianshan Mountains.

2. In the fifth year of Emperor He's reign (93 A.D.), Zhonglang general Ren Shang and Wang Fu led an army to attack the northern Xiongnu monarch to the Eastern Tianshan area.

   This is recorded in the chapter of the *Chronicle of Southern Xiongnu· Book of Later Han*:

   > In the third year (91 A.D.), the northern monarch was defeated by the right lieutenant Geng Kui and fled to an unknown location. His younger brother, KingYu Chujian, established himself as the monarch, and sent thousands of people under King Yu Jian and lord Gu Du to stop at the sea of Pulei, and sent an ambassador to request for the peace.[18] Dou Xian, the great general, submitted a petition to admit the position of Yu Chujian as the northern monarch, and the Han court accepted it. In the fourth year (92 A.D.), Geng Kui was given a seal and ribbon, four jade swords and a feathered lid, and assigned the general Ren Shang as the guardian of the Yiwu, as the previous position of southern Xiongnu monarch. The court wanted to induce to capitulate the northern court, but Dou Xian was killed. In the fifth year, therefore, Yu Chujian rebelled and went back to the north, the Han emperor sent the generals Wang Fu and Ren Shang together with thousands of cavalries to chase after to lure the general back and kill him so as to destroy their power.

   The Eastern Han inscription "Ren Shang Stele" found in Balikun area also records that Ren Shang and Wang Fu captured the northern Xiongnu monarch Yu Chujian in the fifth year of the Yongyuan reign of Emperor He, which also indicates that the northern Xiongnu monarchy was located in the area of Balikun, north of the Eastern Tianshan Mountains at that time.[19]

3. Han Emperor Shun's Yonghe second years (137 A.D.), Dunhuang governor Pei Cen led the army to attack the North Xiongnu King Huyan to the East Tianshan,[20]

---

[18] *The Book of the Later Han·The Biography of Geng Kui* also has a similar record: "the northern monarch brother Yu Chujian establish himself as monarch, the eight tribes of more than 20,000 people live around the Pulei lake".

[19] "Hami Cultural Relics" compilation group: *"Hami Cultural Relics"*, Xinjiang People's Publishing House, 1993.

[20] "Hami Cultural Relics" compilation group: *"Hami Cultural Relics"*, Xinjiang People's Publishing House, 1993.

and the matter is not contained in the history books, but the discovery of "Pei Cen discipline monument" fills the gap in the historical records. The Eastern Han Dynasty inscription "Pei Cen discipline monument" was found in the village of Shirenzi, Shirenzi Town, Balikun County in the seventh year of the Yongzheng era (1725) of the Qing Dynasty, and it is also known as "Zhenhai Stele". The inscription recorded: "at the Han Yonghe second years in August, Dunhuang governor Pei Cen led soldiers 3000 people to crusade against Xiongnu King Huyan, and finally conquered the whole enemy. He protected the western region, and helped to stabilize the border. For this reason, people built the shrine and monument to memorize him for all generations."[21] The discovery site of Pei Cen's stele, Shirenzi Village, is close to the site of the large settlement of Dongheigou, indicating that the site was probably the location of the royal court of King Huyan of the Northern Xiongnu at that time.

The above ancient documents and Han dynasty inscriptions show that a series of large and medium-sized settlement sites of early nomadic culture found in the Eastern Tianshan area should be related to the ruling centres of early nomadic peoples such as the Yuezhi, Wusun and Xiongnu, who were active in the Eastern Tianshan area. The large settlement sites should be the location of the highest ruling centres such as the king's court or monarch's court.

Among the large settlement sites discovered in the Eastern Tianshan area, the Yue Gongtai and Dongheigou sites have been the most archaeologically significant.

The site group of Yue Gongtai and Xiheigou, centred on Lanzhouwanzi, is located in the gently sloping area in front of the northern foothills of East Tianshan Mountain, southwest of Balikun County, and within a range of about 5 km from Yue Gongtai directly south of the county to Xiheigou in the west, there are a series of sites with common cultural characteristics, such as Yue Gongtai, Dazhigou, Wangou, Nijia Ebo, Gaojia Ebo, Lanzhouwanzi, Shuangzha Ebo, so it is named Yue Gongtai-Xiheigou group complex. The complex is about 3 km wide from north to south, and the southern part of the site is between the peaks and valleys of the northern Tianshan Mountains, and the northern part is bounded by the village of Lanzhouwanzi, covering an area of more than 10 km². 1983–1984, the Xinjiang Institute of Cultural Relics and Archaeology excavated the remains of a stone platform at the Lanzhouwanzi site.[22]

From July to August 2002, the Department of Archaeology of Northwestern University investigated and mapped the ground remains of this site group, and found three stone platforms, more than 120 stone enclosures, more than 300 stone burials, and more than 1000 rocks with petroglyphs, which can be confirmed as a large settlement site of ancient nomadic culture.[23] The shape of the petroglyphs is simple and

---

[21] (Qing dynasty) Xu Song and Zhu Yuqi: *"The Waterways of the Western Region"*, China Bookstore, 2005.

[22] "Hami Cultural Relics" compilation group: *"Hami Cultural Relics"*, Xinjiang People's Publishing House, 1993.

[23] Archaeology Department of Northwestern University, Cultural Management Committee of Hami Prefecture: "Survey of the Site Group of Xinjiang Balikun Yegongtai a Xiheigou", *Archaeology and Cultural Relics,* No. 2, 2005.

dull, and the expression is mostly in the form of static outlines with rough lines. The burial form is stone structure, without sealing pile, with a square, rectangular or oval in plan. These rock paintings and burials are widely distributed in eastern Xinjiang and north-western Gansu, representing one types of ancient nomadic culture remains.

Among the cultural remains represented by the Yuegongtai-Xiheigou complex, the excavated ones include the Hanqigou cemetery in Hami[24] and the Baiqier cemetery in Yiwu.[25] From the archaeological data of the cemeteries, it is clear that these remains show the traditional cultural characteristics that continued to develop in the Eastern Tianshan region in the 1st millennium B.C., and they should belong to the local indigenous culture. At the same time, the data also show obvious characteristics of nomadic culture, indicating that the indigenous culture of the region was transformed into nomadic culture at that time.

It is worth noting that the cultural remains represented by the Yuegongtai-Xiheigou group are distributed on the north and south sides of Eastern Tianshan. The settlement sites of this culture distributed in the south side of Eastern Tianshan have a large number of small sites as well as some medium and large sites. The settlement sites of this culture distributed on the northern slope of East Tianshan are only large and medium-sized sites.

In addition to the cultural relics represented by the Yue Gongtai-Xiheigou group, there exists another type of cultural remains from eastern Xinjiang to north-western Gansu. The typical representative of this kind of cultural remains is the Dongheigou site, Balikun County. The Dongheigou site is located in the south of Shirenzi village, which is 23 kms west from Balikun County. From July to September 2005, the Cultural Heritage and Archaeology Research Center of Northwestern University conducted a comprehensive survey and mapping of the site with the assistance of the Cultural Relics Bureau of Hami Prefecture and the Cultural Management Office of Balikun County. The survey found that within the site, which is about 5 km long from north to south, 3.5 km wide from east to west, with an area of 8.75 km^2, there are three large stone platforms, 140 stone enclosures, 1666 burials, and 2485 rocks with petroglyphs, so it is confirmed to be a large scale, rich in connotation, and representative site of ancient nomadic culture. From 2006 to 2007, the Cultural Heritage and Archaeology Research Center of Northwestern University and the Xinjiang Institute of Cultural Relics and Archaeology cooperated in the archaeological excavation of the site, and excavated one of the stone platforms, four stone enclosed dwelling remains, and 12 burials.[26]

---

[24] Xinjiang Institute of Cultural Relics and Archaeology, Hami Regional Cultural Relics Management Institute: "Brief Report of Excavation of Hami Hanqigou Cemetery", *Xinjiang Cultural Relics*, No. 2, 1996.

[25] The burials in the Yiwu Baiqier Cemetery are also square stone tombs with no mounding on the surface. The burial form and the excavated remains are close to the cultural elements of some sites in the Hami Basin since the 1st millennium B.C., such as the Yanbulake Cemetery, the Hanqigou Cemetery, and the Aisikexiaer Cemetery. The excavation data have not been published yet, but the author has had the opportunity to see the unearthed objects from the Baiqier Cemetery in the Hami Museum and has made several field trips to the cemetery.

[26] a. Same as 7.

The obtained archaeological data show that the petroglyphs are mostly carved with metal tools, and the carvings are more delicate and vivid, and the forms of expression are mostly in dynamic outlines. The burial form of this type of cultural remains is a stone structure tomb with round stone seal pile. Due to the space formed by the burial equipment and the filling of large stones in the grave, the middle of the pile is mostly sunken. The small and medium-sized tombs have been excavated, and the pits are rectangular or oval in the east-west direction. The pits of small tombs are shallow, and the burial tools are mostly sarcophagi built with flaky stones. The pits of medium-sized tombs are deeper and mostly use wooden burial tools. Most of the medium-sized tombs have sacrificed horses in the pits, and some tombs have offering pits next to them. In addition to the Dongheigou site, other sites that have been excavated for this type of remains include Balikun Heigouliang Cemetery.[27]

From the available archaeological data, it is clear that these remains are different from those of the culture represented by Yue Gongtai and Xiheigou and represent the culture of a new foreign nomadic people that emerged in the Eastern Tianshan region in the late 1st millennium B.C. Two fragments of bronze mirrors with a feathery ground pattern made in the Central Plains were found in the burial site of Heigouliang Cemetery, which indicates that the emergence of such remains in the Eastern Tianshan region could not be earlier than the end of the Warring States period and the beginning of the Western Han Dynasty. So far, these remains have been found mainly in the area of Balikun and Yiwu to the north of the Eastern Tianshan Mountains, but not in the Hami Basin to the south of the Eastern Tianshan Mountains.

It is noteworthy that both the Dongheigou site and the Heigouliang cemetery found dismembered human remains buried under the burial mounds or in the burial pits, and these skeletons also carried weapons, tools and ornaments, and some even had broken pottery. The features of the relics excavated with the human sacrifice indicate that they belonged to the indigenous culture that continued to develop in the Eastern Tianshan area in the 1st millennium B.C., represented by the Yue Gongtai and Xiheigou site groups. The discovery of a foreign culture represented by the tomb owners and an indigenous culture represented by the human sacrifice at the same site reflects the relationship between the conquerors and the conquered.

This important archaeological discovery, however, dramatically coincides with the documented history of the Xiongnu's defeat of the Yuezhi in the Eastern Tianshan region in the early years of the Western Han Dynasty and their eventual occupation of this region.

---

b. Xinjiang Institute of Cultural Relics and Archaeology, Center for Cultural Heritage and Archaeology, Northwestern University: "2006 Excavations at the Dongheigou Site in Balikun, Xinjiang", *Xinjiang Cultural Relics*, No. 2, 2007.

c. Xinjiang Institute of Cultural Relics and Archaeology, Center for Cultural Heritage and Archaeological Research, Northwestern University, Xinjiang, China: "Brief Report on Excavation of the Dongheigou Site, Balikun County, Xinjiang, 2006–2007," in this issue of this journal.

[27] The excavated materials from the cemetery are now in the Xinjiang Institute of Cultural Relics and Archaeology and the Hami Museum, and are being organized. The author had the opportunity to view the materials in person and assisted in their collation.

Are the remains represented by the Yue Gongtai and Xiheigou group the Yuezhi culture? And the remains represented by the Dongheigou site is the Xiongnu culture? This still needs more archaeological data to prove and test. However, we believe that with the correct methodology and persistent efforts, it is very promising to finally distinguish and confirm the remains of ancient Yuezhi and Xiongnu cultures in the Eastern Tianshan area.

Chapter 5
The 'Venetian' Silver Chalice of Feng Chao 馮朝 *Inventing Medieval Chinese Christianity in Fascist Italy*

Antonio De Caro

Abstract This article tells the story of the unusual 'discovery' of a Chinese silver chalice—the Feng Chao chalice—by the Venetian art collector Gino Spada, the owner of the chalice, and the Jesuit missionary Fr. Pasquale D'Elia S.J. (De Lixian 德禮賢, 1890–1963) between the 1930s and the early 1940s. In particular, it focuses on the epistolary correspondence between D'Elia and Spada concerning the origins of the silver chalice, its use, and its relevance to the history of Sino-European trade along the 'Silk Road(s).' The initial assumption suggested by both authors was that the chalice was produced during the Late Middle Ages in China under the supervision of a European craftsman. In addition, they both hypothesized its Christian origins for it, suggesting that it was probably used by Franciscan missionaries or donated by them to Kublai Khan (Hubilie 忽必烈, 1215–1294) during the Yuan dynasty. This article examines the relevance of this chalice, its 'Christianization', and other contemporary counter-interpretations on its possible origin. In a period of distress and constant changes, the Feng Chao chalice represented a reliable symbol of cross-cultural interaction between Chinese and European culture. This article shows how this imaginative perspective influenced D'Elia and Spada in their initial hypothesis. Finally, it argues that the silver chalice was actually likely produced during the late

---

I would like to express my sincere thanks to the staff of the Archivio Storico della Pontificia Università Gregoriana. I am especially grateful to Mr. Lorenzo Mancini and the Director Fr. Martín M. Morales. I am also immensely grateful to the entire editorial staff of Monumenta Serica, and Dr. Dirk Kuhlmann, in particular, for their support and their efforts. I am also in debt with all the members of the Centre for Early Medieval Studies, Masaryk University in Brno, Czech Republic for their continuous support, especially Dr. Adrien Palladino. This article is the result of the grant research project No. 2020/37/N/HS1/03,273, "Adaptation of the Christian Beliefs of God and Soul in Chinese Thought: Rethinking the Legacy of Early Catholic Missionaries and Converts during 17th-18th Centuries", financed by the National Science Center, Poland (Praca powstała w wyniku realizacji projektu badawczego o nr 2020/37/N/HS1/03273 finansowanego ze środków Narodowego Centrum Nauki).

A. De Caro (✉)
Department of Chinese Studies, Masaryk University, Brno, Czech Republic
e-mail: antonio.decaro@khist.uzh.ch

Centre for Early Medieval Studies, Masaryk University, Brno, Czech Republic

Department of Art History, University of Zurich, Zurich, Switzerland

© SDX Joint Publishing 2023
X. Li (ed.), *Major Archaeological Discoveries Along the Chinese Silk Road*, Silk Road Research Series, https://doi.org/10.1007/978-981-99-0659-8_6

nineteenth century, and was part of a series of several Chinese silverware export goods that were commercialized from Guangzhou to Europe between the late nineteenth century and the early twentieth century.

Keywords Feng Chao chalice · Pasquale D'Elia · Christianity in China · Sino-European exchanges · Silk Road(s) · Venice

5.1 Introduction

The history of Christianity in China during the Middle Ages and the early modern era—including the material exchanges along the 'Silk Roads' between Europe and China—was widely studied during the early and mid-twentieth century.[1] In particular, Fr. Pasquale D'Elia S.J. (De Lixian 德礼贤, 1890–1963) reconstructed both the history of Chinese Christian art[2] and the history of Christianity in China,[3] emphasizing the crucial role played by Roman Catholic missionaries in Sino-European exchange. In an article written in both French and Latin and published in 1930, entitled "Une trouvaille: Un calice catholique chinoise du XIV siècle [Inventum? Calix catholicus sinicus saeculi XIV]" ("A discovery? A Chinese Roman Catholic chalice from the fourteenth century"),[4] he discussed the fascinating, and extremely controversial, discovery of a Chinese silver chalice in Venice, dated to around the fourteenth century that was hypothetically crafted in China with the aid of a European craftsman. In 1932, in direct response to D'Elia's article, Nicola Spada published an article entitled "Il calice di Feng Ch'ao" ("The Chalice of Feng Chao [冯朝]") for the Italian journal *Arte Cristiana* (*Christian art*) in which he stressed the relevance

---

[1] Here it will be provided an extremely concise bibliography, given the narrow scope of the article. See *Opere storiche: del P. Matteo Ricci*, edited by Pietro Tacchi Venturi (Macerata: Giorgetti, 1911–13), 2 vols; *Fonti Ricciane. Documenti Originali Concernenti Matteo Ricci e la Storia delle Prime Relazioni tra l'Europa e la Cina (1579–1615)*, edited by Pasquale M. D'Elia, (Rome: La libreria di Stato, 1942–1949), 3 vols.; Pasquale D'Elia, *Catholic Native Episcopacy in China: Being an Outline of the Formation and Growth of the Chinese Catholic Clergy, 1300–1926*. (Shanghai: T'usewei Press, 1927); Henri Cordier, "Le Christianisme en Chine et en Asie Centrale sous les Mongols" *T'oung Pao*, 18(1/2), (1917), 49–113; Yoshiro P. Saeki, *The Nestorian monument in China* (London: S.P.C.K, 1916); Arthur Christopher Moule, "A Life of Odoric of Pordenone", *T'oung Pao*, 20 (1), (1920), 275–290; Joseph de Moidrey. *La hiérarchie Catholique en Chine, en Corée et au Japon (1307–1914)* (Shanghai: Imprimerie de l'Orphelinat de T'ou-sè-wè, 1914); Louis Pfister, *Notices biographiques et bibliographiques sur les Jésuites de l'ancienne Mission de Chine: 1552–1773* (Shanghai: Imprimerie de la mission catholique, 1932), 2 vols.

[2] Pasquale D'Elia, *Le origini dell'arte cristiana cinese 1583–1640* (Rome: Reale Accademia d'Italia, 1939).

[3] Pasquale D'Elia, *The Catholic missions in China: a short sketch of the history of the Catholic Church in China from the earliest records to our own days*, (Shanghai: The Commercial Press, 1934); Pasquale D'Elia, "I primi albori della luce cattolica in Cina", La Civiltà Cattolica, vol. 4, (1940), 286–300.

[4] Pasquale D'Elia, "Une trouvaille: Un calice catholique chinoise du XIV siècle [Inventum? Calix catholicus sinicus saeculi XIV]", *Collectanea Commissionis Synodalis*, vol. 3, (1930), 715–723.

of this unusual find.[5] The Venetian art collector Gino Spada, Nicola Spada's father, was the owner of this chalice, which had allegedly traveled along the Silk Road(s) connecting Beijing to Venice. As a result, Nicola insisted that this object bridged Chinese culture and European Roman Catholic Christianity during the Middle Ages and represented an important component in the popularization of 'European' Roman Catholicism in the Mongol era (Fig. 5.1).

The Feng Chao chalice is a silver chalice depicting tree main scenes: (1) a convivial scene (Fig. 5.1b), (2) a scene portraying a standing figure surrounded by chivalric (Fig. 5.1a), and (3) a chivalry scene (Fig. 5.5, top right). In the lower section, there are three dragon-like figures surrounding the stem of the chalice. On the inside bottom part of the chalice, there is one inscription carved in Chinese suggesting that the chalice was either produced, owned or manufactured by a person named Feng Chao 馮朝, accompanied by the Latin acronym L. C.

This article will reconstruct the epistolary correspondence between Gino Spada and Pasquale D'Elia concerning this silver chalice. In particular, it will focus on the debate concerning the chalice's 'Christian' iconography. In different ways, both D'Elia and Spada were convinced of the chalice's Christian origin—even though they both acknowledged, more so D'Elia than Spada, the hermeneutic and historical issues with this interpretation.

The reflections on the silver chalice from by D'Elia, Nicola Spada, and Gino Spada on the silver chalice went beyond the object itself, also mirroring the anxiety and the worries of their own time. For Nicola Spada, this was an example of a universal Christian art that was accommodated into the indigenous Chinese culture. For this reason, the chalice represented an ecumenical symbol, especially "looking at the rapid rise of nationalistic movements," and therefore, it was "a fine example of the universality of Christianity also regarding the formation of sacred art".[6]

5.2 The Earliest Description of the Feng Chao Chalice

In his first article on the chalice, published in 1930, D'Elia immediately recognized the difficulty of identifying the use and origin of this object, and even its authenticity. He wrote, "naturally, one wonders: what is this artifact? Assuming that it is authentic and that it is not a forgery—which is impossible to be attested by looking at the [available] photographs [of the object]—could it be a drinking cup (*une coupe à boire/vas potiorum*)? Is it a Catholic chalice (*calice catholique/calix catholicus*)? And if so, when was it produced? Needless to say, no one is currently capable to provide a sound and apodictic answer. All we can do is to suggest more or less well-founded and therefore more or less probable hypotheses".[7] Nevertheless, D'Elia initially

---

[5] Nicola Spada, "Il calice di Feng Ch'ao", *Arte Cristiana,* (1932), 34–38.

[6] Spada, "Il calice di Feng Ch'ao," 36–37.

[7] D'Elia, "Une trouvaille: Un calice catholique chinoise du XIV siècle," 718, translation by the author.

Fig. 5.1 a, **b** 'Feng Chao' silver chalice, photograph, Fondo Pasquale D'Elia, Faldone 14, Fascicolo III, Cartella 8, © Archivio Storico della Pontificia Università Gregoriana

(a)

(b)

Fig. 5.2 'Feng Chao' silver chalice, detail of the bottom indicating the term *Feng Chao ji*馮朝記 (produced or owned by Feng Chao, lit. Feng Chao 'brand'), photograph, Fondo Pasquale D'Elia, Faldone 14, Fascicolo III, Cartella 8, © Archivio Storico della Pontificia Università Gregoriana

suggested that this object could be a *gu dong*古董, an antique and precious object (*res antiqua et pretiosa*). Still, this type of objects was frequently traded by Venetian merchants and travelers ([…] *voyageurs et* […] *merchands/peregrinatores et mercatores*) during the Late Middle Ages. Many wealthy Venetian families, according to D'Elia, still possessed precious objects from that period of exchanges along the 'Silk Roads' during the mid-twentieth century.[8] The chalice represented therefore a very rare or unusual object (*rei rarissimae / un object très curieux*).[9] Interestingly, despite the doubts that arose later in the article, the chalice is presented as follows (Figs. 5.2 and 5.3):

> The vase has the classic shape of Roman Catholic chalices, as it also has their same dimensions (19.6 cm high and 9.4 cm diameter). The pedestal is made of three dragon-headed dolphins. On the base, there are grapes alternately chiseled with vine leaves. The interior is in gilded silver; the gilding is slightly damaged at the top. The lines of the upper edge have a pattern that recalls the Italian art of 1300. At the bottom of the vase, we read: L. C. [*Feng Chao ji*] 馮朝記 (Fig. 5.2).[10]

D'Elia then described the three scenes portrayed on the chalice. The first one, "depicts three armed horsemen and a man sounding the rally with a tam-tam [that is, a gong]" (Fig. 5.5, top right).[11] The second one, showing at the center an official surrounded by other people; "the official is witnessing the leave of a guest. Both the official and his guest seem to have a purse; one person holds it on the left, and the other one on the right" (Fig. 5.5, top left).[12] Yet, according to D'Elia, the third

---

[8] D'Elia, "Une trouvaille: Un calice catholique chinoise du XIV siècle," 715.

[9] D'Elia, "Une trouvaille: Un calice catholique chinoise du XIV siècle," 715.

[10] D'Elia, "Une trouvaille: Un calice catholique chinoise du XIV siècle," 715–716, translation by the author, *modified*.

[11] D'Elia, "Une trouvaille: Un calice catholique chinoise du XIV siècle," 717, translation by the author. Here D'Elia describes the object as a *cymbalo* and a *luo* 鑼 (a gong) adopting an onomatopoeic sound, *dangdang* 鐺鐺.

[12] D'Elia, "Une trouvaille: Un calice catholique chinoise du XIV siècle," 717, translation by the author.

Fig. 5.3 'Feng Chao' silver chalice, detail, photograph, Fondo Pasquale D'Elia, Faldone 14, Fascicolo III, Cartella 8, © Archivio Storico della Pontificia Università Gregoriana

scene is the most significant. In fact, "the most important scene is the one where we see twelve figures sitting around a table covered with a tablecloth. All [the figures] seem to have a gloomy expression. The head of the table occupies the place of honor. Almost in front of him, another character has a sword and seems to be standing up. Vis-à-vis this last character, another one seems to be holding a purse" (Fig. 5.5, center).[13]

From this initial description, D'Elia reached the core of his "working hypothesis"[14]: the chalice might have represented scenes related to Christian iconography and, therefore, could have been produced for liturgical purposes or as a gift for the Khan, probably the Yuan Emperor Kublai Khan (Hubilie 忽必烈, 1215–1294). As a result, the third scene depicted in the chalice could portray the Last Supper. More precisely, it could represent the moment Judas had already left the cenacle.

D'Elia did not attempt to provide a meaning for the two characters L. C. (*dont il nous est impossible de deviner le sens/ quarum sensum interpretari non possumus*).[15] Only in later articles did he propose a possible explanation for the 'mysterious' acronym.

---

[13] D'Elia, "Une trouvaille: Un calice catholique chinoise du XIV siècle," 717–718, translation by the author.

[14] D'Elia, "Une trouvaille: Un calice catholique chinoise du XIV siècle," 719.

[15] D'Elia, "Une trouvaille: Un calice catholique chinoise du XIV siècle," 721.

5.3 Is the Chalice Christian? the Epistolary Correspondence Between D'Elia and Spada

The story of the chalice is clouded by a halo of uncertainty concerning its specific provenance, its use, and even its precise date of production. D'Elia attempted to provide evidence concerning the craftmanship of the object, its periodization and its original use, while being conscious of the difficulty of this task. His main hypothesis—Which was supported by Nicola Spada and was derived from his father's initial conjectures—is that the chalice has been manufactured prior to 1615, given the specific iconography portrayed on it.[16] Following this assumption, D'Elia continued to support the idea that the chalice could have been a gift donated by a Franciscan friar, like Giovanni of Montercorvino (circa 1247–1328), to Kublai Khan.[17] Nicola Spada—like D'Elia—supported the idea that the presence of grapes symbolizing the Eucharist was a clear indication that the chalice was indeed of Christian origin.

Starting from the early 1930s, Gino Spada began to correspond with Pasquale D'Elia regarding the chalice and its Christian elements. For example, in May 1932, Spada had already been asked by a Dominican friar, Giovanni di Martin, to reproduce devotional images of the chalice together with Roman Catholic prayers in Chinese, including the *Lord's Prayer* (*Tianzhu jing* 天主經, Fig. 5.4) and the *Apostles' Creed* (*Xinde tong* 信德誦, Fig. 5.5).[18] These devotional images—including small photographs of the chalice—circulated probably in a circumscribed way among Chinese Christians and European Roman Catholic missionaries who were proficient in Chinese. In a letter dated April 22, 1935, Spada mentioned two similar chalices that he owned, including the Feng Chao chalice, and maintained that the Chinese characters at the bottom of the Feng Chao chalice could provide more substantial evidence regarding its precise periodization—despite the fact that he was presumably not able to read Chinese at all.[19] Spada referred to the Chinese inscription, interpreted by D'Elia as *Feng Chao ji* 馮朝記 (lit. Feng Chao 'brand'):

---

[16] Spada, "Il calice di Feng Ch'ao," 35.

[17] Spada, "Il calice di Feng Ch'ao," 35.

[18] See "Recentemente è stato qui di passaggio il Padre Giovanni di Martin OFM missionario da molti anni in Cina e ritornato per salute, egli ha esaminato l'oggetto e lo ha giudicato un calice cattolico, tanto che mi ha incoraggiato a fare delle immaginette sacre con le scene del calice e una breve preghiera ritenendo possano essere utili in Cina. A questo scopo mi ha fornito il testo del Pater e dell'atto di fede. Mi permetto di accludere qualche copia e alter copie ne ho spedite a S.E Mons. Costantini pregandolo di darmi il suo "nulla osta" per la distribuzione". For the English translation, refer to ""Recently, Father Giovanni di Martin OFM, who had been a missionary in China for several years and returned [to Italy] due to poor health, visited me here. He examined the object and deemed it to be a Roman Catholic chalice and encouraged me to produce devotional images depicting scenes of the chalice attaching a brief prayer to them. For this purpose, he provided me with the text of the Lord's Prayer and the Apostles' Creed. I take the liberty of enclosing a few copies [of them here attached] and I have sent other ones to His Eminence Monsignor Costantini seeking for his permission to distribute them". *Archivio Storico della Pontificia Università Gregoriana (ASPUG)*, Fondo D'Elia 14, III/1, translation by the author. The images are present in *ASPUG, Fondo D'Elia* 14, III/8; one of them is preserved in *ASPUG, Fondo D'Elia* 14, III/9.

[19] *ASPUG, Fondo D'Elia*, 14, III/3.

Fig. 5.4 Reproduction of a detail of the 'Feng Chao chalice' including the *Lord's prayer* in Chinese, print, Fondo Pasquale D'Elia, Faldone 14, Fascicolo III, Cartella 9, © Archivio Storico della Pontificia Università Gregoriana

Concerning the mark (*marca*) that has been inscribed in the chalice and that has got three bamboos at its base, I was not able to reproduce it. Firstly, the incision is not deep enough – since it has been rather consumed by the time – and secondly it can be reproduced only upside-down. As a result, I decided to take a second photograph with an enlargement that is just two times the natural size, and in this way it could be clearer than the previous one that I sent to You[...]. You can find it here attached. So, if you look at it with an enlargement lens, I hope you would be able to decipher [this signature] since this would be a decisive element to comprehend the precise period in which the Chalice of the Last Supper [was produced]. In fact, in both chalices there is that shield [...] that You were already able to recognize.[20]

The epistolary correspondence between D'Elia and Spada continued, and it followed a very detailed exchange of information between the two sides. Unfortunately, only the letters from Spada have been preserved and we cannot consider the responses provided by D'Elia who, according to Spada, seemed very interested in the object and in its specific significance for the exchange and production of Christian artifacts during the fourteenth century. In November 1940, D'Elia received another letter from Gino Spada—after sending him a letter on October 30—who capably tried to convince him of the relevance of the chalice as a Christian object produced in China. In order to corroborate this hypothesis, Spada pointed out another important

---

[20] *ASPUG, Fondo D'Elia*, 14, III/3. Translation by the author.

5 The 'Venetian' Silver Chalice of Feng Chao 馮朝 *Inventing* …

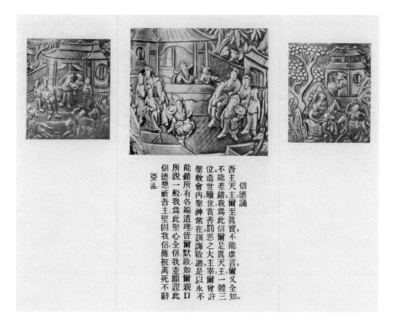

Fig. 5.5 Reproduction of the three main scenes of the 'Feng Chao chalice' including the *Apostles' Creed* in Chinese, print, Fondo Pasquale D'Elia, Faldone 14, Fascicolo III, Cartella 9, © Archivio Storico della Pontificia Università Gregoriana

detail that, in his opinion, clearly showed that the chalice was produced in China under the guidance of a European craftsman. The characters L. C.—the aforementioned Latin acronym—were inscribed on the bottom part of the chalice. This particular element gave Spada the opportunity to fantasize on the possible origin of the chalice and to reflect on the specific disposition of the horsemen in the chivalric scene. At the same time, the letter demonstrates the struggle Spada had in reconstructing the importance of the scene and its precise periodization:

> Dear Reverend Father,
>
> I thank You for Your letter [that I received on] the 30th of the previous month. Please accept my dearest apologies for my belated reply since I have been particularly busy during the last few days.
>
> The photograph that I sent to you, showing the two letters L. C., is not particularly clear and I also personally, when I saw it, was not able to see the two letters one so close to the other. However, if You observe the photograph looking at it in a way in which the mark is on the observer's left, You will be able to see more clearly the two letters L. C., close to each other. They are dark and surrounded by a brighter background.
>
> Concerning the upper part of the chalice—that I mentioned when You were still in Shanghai—a Venetian architect told me that the disposition of the lines was very similar to what was used during the 1300s. However, I did not receive any further news about this.
>
> Observing the series of horsemen going around almost the entire chalice, it seems that they are very peculiar figures, and their posture is extremely original. As a result, they could have not been crafted by an artist who did not have a first sight to the real vision of horsemen.

Once I take photographs of this specific scene, I will send a copy of them to You. Given your great expertise on Chinese art, You will be able to offer me your judgment.

A few days ago I also wrote a letter to His Excellence Celso Costantini [1876–1958] thanking Him for his mention of the chalice in the last monograph that he wrote. I took this opportunity to ask him whether he had any further evidence to suppose that the chalice was dated around 1600. Given the fact that His Excellence is particularly kind and seeing that I did not receive any answer from him yet, I believe that his judgment was solely based on a personal impression [of the object].

I sincerely apologize to You, Father, since I wasted your time with my words. Please receive my beloved and devout greetings to You.

Yours truly,

Gino Spada[21]

In the same year, in an article named *"I primi albori della luce Cattolica in Cina"* (*"The first dawning of the Roman Catholic light in China"*), D'Elia mentioned, once again, the potential relevance of the chalice for the history of Christianity in China during the Yuan dynasty. Here, D'Elia pointed out a possible solution for deciphering the acronym L. C. According to him, a probable meaning of the acronym was *Latinus Calix* (Latin Chalice) distinguishing it from other, as he defined them, "'Nestorian' [Christian] chalices".[22] Here, he presented the chalice very concisely and suggested that the chalice 'seemed' to be a Christian object crafted during the Yuan dynasty in China. In addition, D'Elia—not dissimilarly from the initial hypothesis by Nicola Spada—suggested that the grapes on the chalice's surface probably suggested that it was used for the Mass and other liturgical purposes.

5.4 A Different Perspective on the Chalice

D'Elia and Spada—in different ways—proposed just one possible solution on the origin of the Feng Chao chalice, also encompassing its possible use and its iconography. Another possibility, apart from the idea that it was a contemporary forgery of a 'Medieval' silver chalice, was that it was not actually related to Christianity at all, but that both D'Elia and Spada forced the interpretation of the iconography, accommodating it to their initial assumption.

In 1933, D'Elia was probably seeking another opinion on the relevance of the object and its 'Christian' iconography. As a result, he sent to John Calvin Ferguson (Fu Kaisen 福開森, 1866–1945), an American scholar and expert in Chinese art, a few photographs of the Feng Chao chalice. After careful analysis, Ferguson maintained that the object was probably inspired by Chinese traditional folklore and culture and was not related to any possible 'Christian' iconography, especially any evangelical scene. The letter dated October 9, 1933, he sent to D'Elia challenges D'Elia's initial assumption, supporting a non-Christian origin and use for the chalice:

---

[21] *ASPUG, Fondo D'Elia,* 14, III/6. Translation by the author.

[22] Pasquale D'Elia, "I primi albori della luce cattolica in Cina," 295, f. 1.

Dear Father D'Elia,

Your letter dated October 4th reached me on the 7th and yesterday I received the registered cover enclosing a copy of *Arte Cristiana* and the *Digest of the Synodal Commission* containing the article published concerning the chalice. The package also contained three photographs, but I found that the illustrations in *Arte Cristiana* are quite as good as the photographs.

The scene depicted on the cup is fully described in *Sao Kuo Yen I* (三國演義) vol. 7, the number of the play being 56 (第五十六回). The subject of this play is the feast at T'ung Ch'iao T'ai given by Ts'ao Ts'ao (曹操大宴銅雀臺). The first view is that to the left on p. 36 of *Arte Cristiana* in which a man seated on a horse with a bow in his hand is facing another horseman advancing with drawn bow. This is Chang Ho (張郃) who had hit the target by shooting backward whereas the other archers were shooting straight ahead. The man beating the drum above is acclaiming the fact that the target was hit. The second scene is that on the right side of this page and shows Ts'ao Ts'ao watching the contest.

As you will see after you have read the text, a controversy arose between Hsu Huang (徐晃) and Hsu Ch'u (許褚) as to the prize and Ts'ao Ts'ao is seated behind a table making peace between the two contestants. According to the narrative Ts'ao Ts'ao arranged the partizans in two rows on either side of the table and adjudicated the controversy, as shown in the third scene.

Not having seen the cup I have no idea as to when it was made by the story depicted is well-known on the Chinese stage and familiar to the theatre goers. The three Chinese characters which are said to be carved on the inside of the vase, viz. *Feng Ch'ao Chi* (馮朝記) probably indicated the name of the workman who designed the cup or the name of the shop which sold it.

I am retaining the material which you sent me together with the photographs but will return them to you if you so desire.

With kindest regards,

Yours sincerely,

John C. Ferguson[23]

We are not completely aware of D'Elia's reactions to Ferguson's letter; yet, in the following years, D'Elia, as mentioned earlier, continued to support his initial hypothesis that the chalice was probably connected to fourteenth-century Franciscan missions. For Ferguson, the chivalric scene is directly related to the *Romance of the Three Kingdoms* (*Sanguo Yanyi* 三國演義). Similarly, it was also difficult for Ferguson to reconstruct the period in which the object was produced, but he agrees with D'Elia that it was probably produced by a craftsman named Feng Chao, based on the mark of the object.

5.5 Epilogue: The War and the Chalice

Fascist Italy joined the Second World War against the Allies, supporting the Axis alliance, on June 10, 1940. The following year, the epistolary correspondence between D'Elia and Spada became sporadic and then, eventually, ceased. On

---

[23] ASPUG, *Fondo D'Elia*, 14, III/15. The letter has been originally written in English.

November 8, 1941, D'Elia received another letter from Spada.[24] Here, for the very first time since he started correspondence with the Jesuit missionary, Spada acknowledged that his interest in the chalice had been jeopardized by the unstable and dramatic situation in Europe. Intriguingly, the American ambassador in Italy, William Phillips (1878–1968), became particularly interested in the object and offered Spada twenty thousand American dollars on behalf of an unnamed wealthy American individual. The Venetian art collector immediately rejected the offer and continued his efforts to find more information on the chalice and its economic and cultural value. From this moment on, no more substantial information concerning the Feng Chao chalice

---

[24] See. "Most Reverend and Dearest Father, It has been several months since I came to bother You with my letters. I was for three months experiencing the peacefulness of our little house at Alberoni di Lido and then in our villa at Refrontolo, just as quiet as the little house, where, with peace in our hearts, we live very well. Three days ago, I returned to Venice. I am also kindly asking You to write to me if Your two-volume book on Father Ricci is already printed and whether it is already on sale and at what price. I wrote to Cavalier De Angelis on May 13 of this year begging him to obtain three extracts of '*I primi albori della luce cattolica*' printed on my behalf, but I had no reply. Should I write back to him once again? I have never written to You about this. Recently I sent a photograph of the Chalice to the director of the Field Museum of Chicago in December 1938. I received a reply from the director of the Field Museum of Natural History, Mr. Clifford C. Gregg, in order to have his opinion [on the chalice]. In fact, I believed that in his museum it was preserved the famous [replica of the] *Madonna of Santa Maria Maggiore*, but perhaps there are two Field Museums in Chicago. He proposed me to contact two very competent individuals in Chinese art: Dr. Paul Pelliot [1878–1945], in Paris, and Mr. Arthur Christopher Moule [1873–1957] in Cambridge, England. Have you ever heard of these two gentlemen? Afterwards, the American Consul in Venice paid me a visit. He asked me to show him the chalice and after having examined it, he told me whether I wanted to sell it to a rich American [entrepreneur] who was willing to buy it, offering me a very generous amount: 20 thousand [American] dollars. I answered him that I could not deprive myself of such a valuable object. Later—since I was seeking for an opinion on the value of the chalice—I wrote to an English Office. [This same office] had previously made me an estimate of a painting by an English painter, since I own [it] in my small collection of paintings, namely 'The Connoiseur' located at 28–30 Grosvenor Gardens, London. [The Equiry Manager of the 'Connoiseur'] replied on January 22, 1940:
 '*Dear Sir, We fear we shall be unable to deal with your enquiry, because there is no means of arriving at the market value of a piece which is unique, other than placing it under the hammer and waiting to see what it will fetch.*
 With many regrets, Yours faithfully, […] *Enquiry Manager*'.
 This letter was already stamped in the following way: '*Opened by Censor 1157*'. I replied that I didn't want to have a precise price – I was just interested in knowing [the estimated] value [of the chalice]. I received their answer on '*April 26th 1940*':
 '*The Connoiseur. Dear Sir, In reply to your letter of the 16th inst. Our expert regrets that it would be impossible for him to form an estimation of the value of the piece you mention. Yours faithfully, Asked Enquiry Manager*'.
 And this one was signed as follows: '*Opened by examiner 1612*'. Unfortunately [as you can see], the war—that destroyed so much wealth—had already broken out. Please excuse me, Father, if I have bored You with this letter of mine. If you will be so kind to answer me, I will be most grateful to You. Remember me sometimes and please accept my most cordial and cordial greetings. To you servant, Gino Spada".
 ASPUG, *Fondo D'Elia* 13, III/5, translation by the author; the text in italics is in English in the original letter.

is present in scholarship. This letter is therefore the last one available that is directly addresses the relevance of the object and the struggles faced by Spada.

Even though D'Elia continued to mention the relevance of the discovery of the Feng Chao chalice in his works—especially in his *Fonti Ricciane* (*Sources on [Matteo] Ricci*, 1942–1949)[25]—this moment represented the end of further discussions or academic studies on the object. Just like it appeared abruptly in 1930, so the chalice rapidly disappeared almost completely from the general debates on Christianity in China in the 1940s.

In the same period, especially between 1931 and 1937, D'Elia, as shown by Sergio Palagiano, had another epistolary exchange with Fr. Pietro Tacchi Venturi S.J. (1861–956) concerning the new edition of Venturi's *Opere storiche del P. Matteo Ricci S. I.* (*Historical works of Fr. Matteo Ricci S.J.*).[26] This correspondence ended with the sudden decision by Tacchi Venturi not to publish the new edition of his previous two-volume book, originally published between 1911 and 1913. D'Elia then decided to publish Ricci's historical sources in his *Fonti Ricciane*. As mentioned by Palagiano, a possible cause of the decision by Tacchi Venturi to interrupt his commitment to publish a new edition of Ricci's works was his role as a mediator between Pope Pius XI (1857–1939) and Benito Mussolini (1883–1945) on different crucial issues, including the education of the youth and the definition of 'racial practices' after the promulgation of the notorious fascist Italian racial laws (*Leggi Razziali*) from 1938 to 1943.[27]

During this period, D'Elia imagined—together with Spada—that the Feng Chao chalice was a unique object which traveled along the 'Medieval Silk Road(s)' connecting Venice to Beijing, the Mediterranean world to China. Despite the clear doubts that D'Elia had on the authenticity of the chalice starting in 1930, he was willing to support its Christian origin as a working hypothesis. This happened in a crucial period for D'Elia's life and works. He came back to Rome in 1936 after a long missionary period in Shanghai. Subsequently, his efforts on Ricci's works lead

---

[25] See "To the aforesaid recollection, which is generally accepted, one can perhaps add, if authentic, a chalice of 19.6 cm. in height and 9.4 cm. in diameter, which was found in Venice and is now owned by a Venetian, a passionate lover of ancient things, [named] Mr. Gino Spada. On the cup you can see a scene that made one think of the Last Supper, with twelve characters, some of whom have bearded faces and therefore rather Mongolian than Chinese, around a table, and dressed, one would say, in Mongolian style; even the decoration seems, at least in part, Mongolian. That the chalice at some point in its history was in China, is certain from the Chinese inscription Fomciao chi 馮朝記 that is, 'made' or 'owned by Mr. Fomciao [Feng Chao]', which can be read on the bottom of the base of the chalice. That it is a chalice for the celebration of Mass could be deduced from the bunches of grapes, alternating with vine leaves, carved on the cup. The fact that it was made under the eyes of a European is evident from the inscription L. C. which accompanies the Chinese inscription. In any case, the Mongolian style and the houses adopting a typical Mongolian architecture suggest the era of the Mongols, and therefore that of the first mission of the Franciscans", *Fonti Ricciane*, v. 1, LXXIV, translation by the author.

[26] Sergio Palagiano, "Il carteggio tra Pietro Tacchi Venturi e Pasquale D'Elia per la nuova edizione delle Opere storiche del P. Matteo Ricci," *Idomeneo*, n.30, (2020), 59–90.

[27] Palagiano, "Il carteggio tra Pietro Tacchi Venturi e Pasquale D'Elia per la nuova edizione delle Opere storiche del P. Matteo Ricci," 60–61.

him to consolidate his position as a renowned scholar for the study of the history of Christianity in China even more. Surrounded by the winds of war, D'Elia and Spada imagined the previous periods of interactions between China and Europe during the fourteenth century as a vibrant period of commercial, cultural and religious exchanges. The chalice was a symbol of Roman Catholicism becoming a global religion—or as Nicola Spada wrote, "a fine example of the universality of Christianity". Their epistolary exchange shows the efforts that both D'Elia and Spada made in order to 'Christianize' this silver chalice. Spada struggled to comprehend the value of this object and its relevance for the history of Sino-European interactions, or even Christianity in China. Yet, the 'Silk Road(s)' became an imaginary place where the silver chalice was the material symbol of peaceful commercial and artistic interactions between the Mediterranean world and the Chinese empire.

Around the same time D'Elia was set to return to Europe, the Italian poet Cesare Pavese was pondering his poetic inspirations. In this moment of intense reflection, he wrote in his journal in 1935:

> Why cannot I write about these red, moonlit cliffs? Because they reflect nothing of myself. The place gives me a vague uneasiness, nothing more, and that should never be sufficient justification for a poem. If these rocks were in Piedmont, though, I could very well absorb them into a flight of fancy and give them meaning. Which comes to the same thing as saying that the fundamental basis of poetry may be a subconscious awareness of the importance of those bonds of sympathy, those biological vagaries, that are already alive, in embryo, in the poet's imagination before the poem is begun.[28]

Similarly, the Feng Chao chalice became a source of inspiration, an almost poetic one, to both its owner and D'Elia; it was an element that mirrored the beauty of cross-cultural encounter in a period of distress. The absence of meaning was then replaced by a sense of belonging to a distant past—a moment of interaction and exchange connecting the Eurasian continent. The chalice reconnected a breaking reality, it became, for a short while, an imaginative sign of the trading routes connecting distant worlds, recreated by an unusual discovery.

Appendix: A Possible Solution to the Riddle of the Feng Chao Chalice

Pasquale D'Elia and Gino Spada emphasized the relevance of the Feng Chao chalice as a 'Christian' artifact produced in China during the fourteenth century. The same object, traveling across the commercial routes of the Eurasian continent, reached Venice in an undetermined period. Despite their analysis and their interesting surmises, my hypothesis is that the silver chalice was probably produced around the late nineteenth century. For example, a silver mug produced in 1870 circa (Fig. 5.6) has precisely the same carved marks as the ones found on the Feng Chao chalice

---

[28] Cesare Pavese, *This Business of Living: Diaries 1935–1950*, edited by John Taylor (London: Routledge, 2009), 11.

5 The 'Venetian' Silver Chalice of Feng Chao 馮朝 Inventing … 83

Fig. 5.6 Chinese Export Silver Mug, © S& J Stodel, London, United Kingdom, private collection, 1870 circa

(Fig. 5.7). According to the private owner of this mug, the mark L. C. does not indicate a Latin acronym, but rather the romanization of the Chinese name Li Sheng 利升, who was an important retailer in Guangzhou, as 'Leeching', hence L. C. The mark in Chinese denotes the maker of the object, namely Feng Chao. The presence of several other romanized acronyms on similar mugs suggests that the chalice was distributed by Li Sheng in the late nineteenth century and then probably reached Venice probably in the early twentieth century. Another example is a Chinese silver export punch bowl dated around 1875 with three dragon-like figures similar to the ones of the Feng Chao chalice at its base (Fig. 5.8).

Similar objects, including hunting trophies, reached Hong Kong during the early colonial period. Huang Chao analyzed one of those objects called the 'Hunters Plate', dated around 1846 in detail. The object also depicts hunting scenes. In this case, Huang suggests that the object followed a well-established British model, and it cannot be understood as a Chinese silver export good.[29] Interestingly—similarly to the first hypothesis by Ferguson in 1933 concerning the Feng Chao chalice—for Huang this trophy could have been inspired by the *Romance of the Three Kingdoms*:

> The body of the trophy is, in turn, a veritable cornucopia of Chinese and Western Neo-classical motifs transmuted onto the pure Western form. Had this not been Chinese, it would, in any case, exemplify the Victorian love of over-embellishment and the general disregard of the strict limits that other Western stylistic periods tended to have. The motifs on the trophy are both traditional Chinese and, on analysis, interestingly suited to their use on a horse-racing prize.

---

[29] Refer to Huang Chao, "A Qing Dynasty, Silver Racing Trophy from Early Colonial Hong Kong," *Journal of the Royal Asiatic Society Hong Kong Branch*, vol. 58 (2018), 137–153.

Fig. 5.7 Chinese Export Silver Mug, detail of the marks indicating the acronym L. C. and the signature *Feng Chao ji* 馮朝記, © S& J Stodel, London, United Kingdom, private collection, 1870 circa

Fig. 5.8 Unidentified maker (Chinese, 19th century) Punch Bowl with Battle Scene and Dragons c. 1875, silver © Huntington Museum of Art, Huntington, West Virginia. Gift of Herbert Fitzpatrick 1952.296

In the Qing Dynasty, the flourishing of Canton stimulated the development of traditional operas. Both local and non-local operas were popular among citizens. Some of the figures and military scenes from the operas were adopted and recorded in nineteenth-century watercolour-pith export paintings as well as on porcelains and silverware. Other scenes from famous Chinese classics or traditional novels like *The Investiture of Gods* and *The Romance of the Three Kingdoms* also feature. The trophy is no exception.[30]

---

[30] Huang, "A Qing Dynasty, Silver Racing Trophy from Early Colonial Hong Kong," 148.

As a result, the Feng Chao chalice could be one of those objects, produced probably in Guangzhou around the late nineteenth century and circulated in Hong Kong, and then in Europe. Nevertheless, the Feng Chao chalice represents an important and curious example of the imagination of Pasquale D'Elia on the exchanges across Eurasia during the Late Middle Ages. Even though this is probably a later nineteenth century chalice, it is not entirely impossible that Roman Catholic artifacts could have been produced at the very beginning of the period of exchange between European and Chinese cultures. This possibility led D'Elia and Spada to formulate the hypothesis that it could have been a fourteenth century chalice produced in China under the supervision of a European craftsman. This is probably extremely unlikely—but the impression sparked the curiosity of several individuals who were seeking objects that traveled across Eurasia during the Late Middle Ages and then reached Venice. This quest still continues today.

Bibliography

Archivio Storico della Pontificia Università Gregoriana (ASPUG), Fondo D'Elia, 13, III, 5; 14, III, 1–15

Chao H (2018) A Qing Dynasty, silver racing trophy from early Colonial Hong Kong. J Roy Asiatic Soc Hong Kong Branch 58:137–153

D'Elia P (1930) Une trouvaille: Un calice catholique chinoise du XIV siècle [Inventum? Calix catholicus sinicus saeculi XIV] (A discovery? A Chinese Catholic chalice from the 14th century). Collectanea Commissionis Synodalis, Beijing, pp 715–723

D'Elia P (1934) The catholic missions in China: a short sketch of the history of the Catholic Church in China from the earliest records to our own days. The Commercial Press, Shanghai

D'Elia P (1939) Le origini dell'arte cristiana cinese 1583–1640. Reale Accademia d'Italia, Rome

D'Elia P (1940) I primi albori della luce cattolica in Cina. La Civiltà Cattolica IV:286–300

D'Elia P (ed) (1942–1949) Fonti Ricciane. Documenti Originali Concernenti Matteo Ricci e la Storia delle Prime Relazioni tra l'Europa e la Cina (1579–1615), vol. 3. La libreria di Stato, Rome.

Palagiano S (2020) Il carteggio tra Pietro Tacchi Venturi e Pasquale D'Elia per la nuova edizione delle Opere storiche del P. Matteo Ricci. Idomeneo 30:59–90

Tacchi Venturi P (ed) (1911–13) Opere storiche: del P. Matteo Ricci, vol 2. Giorgetti, Macerata

Chapter 6
A Comparative Study of Layouts of Buddhist Monasteries in Gandhāra Area and Tarim Basin

Xiao Li and Zhitang Liao

Abstract This paper focuses on the comparison between layouts of Buddhist monasteries from Gandhāra and Tarim Basin, two significant areas of Buddhist prosperity along the Silk Road from third century B.C. on. Originated from ancient India, Buddhism including its architectural art have localized and innovated itself when it touched various peoples, cultures and religions, which can be seen in developments of main stūpa and pool in the courtyard. While circular stūpa base gradually gave way to square one with its elevation in vertical direction, pool in the central courtyard became dispensable and decorative from India, Gandhāra, Central Asia to western regions area. The whole monasteries developed a more organized and enclosed pattern, reflecting not only harmony in architecture design but also contradicts among different classes and beliefs changes in Buddhism practice.

Keywords Buddhist monastery · Layouts · Gandhāra · Tarim Basin comparative study

6.1 Introduction

The geographic scope involved in this paper extends across Central Asia and northern South Asia, mainly covering Pamir Mountains, India, Pakistan, Afghanistan, Uzbekistan, Kyrgyzstan and areas around Tarim Basin in Xinjiang, China (Fig. 6.1).

Soon after its birth and initial development in India, Buddhism gradually developed another religious center in Greater Gandhāra, which refers to northwestern frontier of India mainly including four areas of Taxila, Peshāwar, Swāt and Kashmir.[1] From here, Buddhism was transmitted into Afghanistan, crossing Amur Darya to

X. Li (✉)
Renmin University of China, Haidian Disctrict, Beijing, China
e-mail: haidaoqi@aliyun.com

Z. Liao
Chinese Academy of Social Sciences, Chaoyang District, Beijing, China

[1] R. Salmon, *Ancient Buddhist Scrolls from Gandhāra: The British Library Kharoṣṭhī Fragments*, Seattle: University of Washington Press, 1999, pp. 3–5, Map. 1.

© SDX Joint Publishing 2023
X. Li (ed.), *Major Archaeological Discoveries Along the Chinese Silk Road*,
Silk Road Research Series, https://doi.org/10.1007/978-981-99-0659-8_7

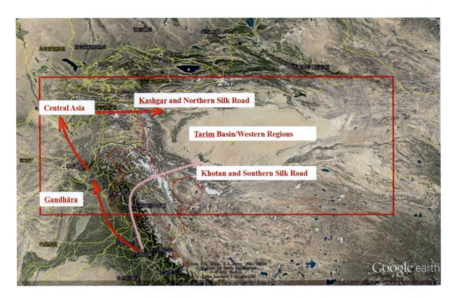

Fig. 6.1 Map of areas involved in the spread of Buddhism from Gandhāra to Tarim Basin[2]

Transoxiana and around third or fourth century A.D., after traveling beyond Pamir Plateau, reached the oasis city of Kashgar in northwestern Tarim Basin while another branch of Buddhism might have arrived at oasis city of Khotan in southwestern Tarim Basin across Karakoram Mountain at an earlier period. As spreading its religious doctrine and texts, Buddhism also spread its influence via religious paintings, sculptures and architectures. Buddhism tried to incorporate local cultural elements everywhere it traveled, and therefore, even within Central Asia, Buddhist art including its architectural part demonstrated not only Indian ingredients but also more distinctly, miscellaneous ethnic characteristics of Persia, Greece and so on. All these artistic diversities showed us the various geographical regions and historical periods where Buddhism has left its traces. From fourth or fifth century A.D. on, Buddhist pilgrims from central plain of ancient China such as Fa Xian, Xuan Zang and Song Yun tried to go westward seeking after Buddhist dharma. Their travel routes also reflected the complicated transportation networks linking the northwestern India, Afghanistan and Tarim basin back then.[3]

In northwestern India and Central Asia, Buddhist architectures first appeared around third century B.C. They were early stūpas that preserved the Buddha's relics, residing rooms in form of ārāmas and stone pillars with carved inscriptions of orders, which exist in small number in southern Afghanistan, northern Pakistan and Central.[4] Since Kushan Dynasty has integrated a vast land, Buddhist architectures and statues

---

[2] The Original Map came from Google Earth. (Last assessed on 2022/4/5).

[3] Sh. Kuwayama, "Pilgrimage Route Changes and the Decline of Gandhāra," in Pia Brancaccio and Kurt A. Behrendt eds., *Gandhāran Buddhism*, Vancouver: UBC Press, 2006, pp. 107–134.

[4] H. Sarkar, *Studies in Early Buddhist Architecture of India*, New Delhi: Oriental Publishers, 1966, pp. 1–14.

had been created in large number and transmitted in large area. The history of development can be divided into three phases: The first phase is Kushan Dynasty period from first to third century A.D. when architectures were distributed largely in Gandhāra proper area, Peshāwar as the center. There were also some Buddhist architectures scattered in Termez near the southern border of Uzbekistan and the north bank of Amu Darya especially around Surkhan Darya. The second phase is post-Kushan period from fourth or fifth century A.D. when Buddhist architectures started to lessen. They were mainly built at Merv in Turkmenistan and Bāmiyān in central Afghanistan. The third phase is the Turkish period and flourishing Tang period from sixth to eighth A.D. century when Buddhist architecture were still flourishing in northern-central Afghanistan and Ferghana valley.[5]

Chronologies of Buddhist ruins found around Tarim Basin differ greatly. For example, based on C-14 data, the main stūpa within the northern stūpa-forest (Talin, 塔林) of Ancient Jiaohe City Ruins (Jiaohe Gucheng, 交河故城) in Turfan can be dated back to East Han Dynasty around the Christian era, while the grottoes along the northern Tarim basin were not built until third or fourth century A.D. This indicates the complicated transmission routes of the Buddhism into Tarim Basin.

Through a comparative study of layouts of Buddhist monasteries discovered in the above-mentioned areas, this article aims to clarify the stable factors that remained for long in historical development as well as the local cultural factors that influenced the Buddhist architectures. Hopefully, the research of Buddhist architecture and Buddhism itself could be improved.

6.2 Gandhāra Buddhism and Layouts of Buddhist Monasteries

Gandhāra was once a land of Buddhism prosperity from third century B.C. to eighth century A.D. Today, there are still many Buddhist ruins in existence across this area (Fig. 6.2). Generally speaking, Gandhāran Buddhist monasteries consist of basically two parts: stūpa court for worshipping stūpa and vihāra court for Buddhists' residence, in some cases two parts integrated into one courtyard. As an important creation by Gandhāran Buddhism in the first several centuries after the Christian era, such pattern has spread north to Afghanistan and Central Asia, east to Tarim Basin and even into central plain of ancient China and East Asia.[6]

---

[5] Education Department of State Administration of Cultural Heritage ed., *Summary of Archaeology of Buddhist Grottoes* (in Chinese), Beijing: Cultural Relics Press, 1993, p. 246.

[6] Above the Yungang Cave hilltop in Datong, Shanxi Province of mainland China, archeologist completely discovered and cleared a ground monastery as early as Beiwei (北魏) period that combined the stūpa court into the vihāra court. The complete archaeological report has recently come out. See Yungang Academy, Shanxi Provincial Institute of Archaeology and Datong Municipal Institute of Archaeology, *Excavation Report of Buddhist Temple ruins at Hilltop of Yungang Grottoes*, I-III, Beijing: Cultural Relics Press, 2021.

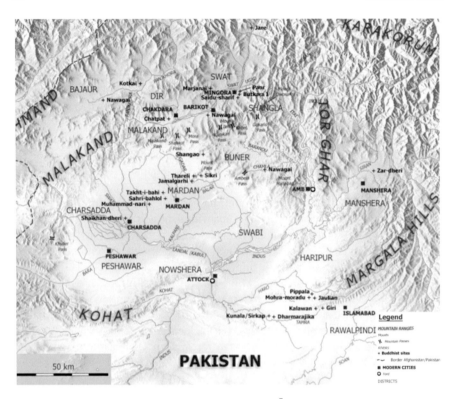

Fig. 6.2 Map of distributions of Buddhist sites in Gandhāra[7]

Before the Kushan Dynasty, stūpas mainly stand as a low structure shaped in reversed bowl. This is typical of stūpas of early period in central India. Remnants of stone railings around the stūpas can still be seen to create the circumambulatory path for religious rituals. Not far from the circle-based main stūpa usually located a line or lines of square-shaped dwelling unit of the monks or nuns. During the Kushan period, Buddhist stūpa were commonly in shape of reversed bowl with a square base faced with sculptures in decoration and above it was a cylindrical stūpa body sustaining a reversed-bowl-shaped structure. The early reversed bowl gradually became taller. Stūpas of such kind existed in Gandhāra, Central Asia and western regions (ancient Xinjiang, "西域"). In second century A.D., under the reign of Kaniṣka and Huvishka, another new mode of Buddhist stūpa was developed to become the mainstream, that is square-based and multi-story stūpa. These changes of the architectural form of stūpa suggest the increasing complexity of Buddhist rituals in Gandhāra area ever since first century A.D.

---

[7] W. Rienjang and P. Stewart eds., *The Geography of Gandhāran Art: Proceedings of the Second International Workshop of the Gandhāra Connections Project,* 2019, vi–vii.

In this part, a comparative study will be conducted on the layouts of three well-preserved Buddhist sites, Dharmarājikā Buddhist complex and Jauliañ monastery in Taxila, and Takht-i-Bāhī monastery in Peshawar.

Dharmarājikā Buddhist Complex, besides the northern vihāras area excavated by Khan Sahib A. D. Siddiqi,[8] mainly consists of a vast worship area including the Dharmarājikā Stūpa as the main stūpa, plenty of votive stūpas and Buddhist shrines cleared under the direction of J. Marshall (Fig. 6.3). Based on numismatic and masonry evidence, Dharmarājikā Stūpa is thought to be built in second century B.C., and the whole Buddhist complex went through enlargement for several times till around sixth century A.D. Even today, remnants of railings around the circumambulating path dated from the very initial construction period can still be seen (Fig. 6.4).

The circular pedestal of Dharmarājikā Stūpa was built of stone, with a diameter of 46 m and stairways in four directions. Such reversed-bowl-shaped structure was recorded clearly by *Mahāsaṅgha Vinaya*, "then Buddha himself built a stūpa with square pedestal, with surrounding railings (Lanshun, "栏楯"), twofold structure, protruded rectangular platforms (Fangya, "方牙"). Above the stūpa is canopies (Pangai, "盘盖") and wheels of dharma (Lunxiang, "轮相")".[9] Here, the so-called four out-forward platforms refer to the rectangular platforms found around the stūpa pedestal which were connected with the circumambulating path by stairways (Fig. 6.5). The Dharmarājikā stūpa was face with stone pieces with stone body inside in particular shape of wheel. Although the reversed-bowl already collapsed with time but its remaining part still stands about 15 m tall, reminding of the greatness and grand scale back then. Around the Dharmarājikā Stūpa are six vihāra courts with main stūpas insides and several additionally built votive stūpas that reflected different phrases of Buddhist monasteries. All these worshipping and dwelling architectures were initially arranged coordinated and harmonized in small numbers, but then became disorderly as an increasing number of architectures fulfilled all the available space in-between.

From its layouts, the northern monastery was first built in early Kushan period, later than the Dharmarajīka Stūpa. Still in well-preserved condition, it consists of five vihāra court centered upon a square-pedestal stūpa with a number of rooms around. The vihāra courts are all square in plan, with only one narrow gate opened in the south wall, just the same size of a vihāra, which may imply the strict disciplines (vinaya). Rooms were set up in line close to or around a spacious courtyard usually with a central square pool designed for bathing (Fig. 6.6). Buddhist architecture of this kind of layouts and structure was thought to first appear in Taxila in the first century. Yet according to professor Li Chongfeng, to the northwest of this whole vihāra court was a square site, part of which was obviously broken by the former. This means the monastery was likely to be later built than the square site in later Gandhāra period.

---

[8] Khan Sahib A. D. Siddiqi, "Excavations at Taxila," *Archaeological Survey of India, Annual Report 1934–1935,* pp. 28–31, Pls. v–viii; "Excavations at Taxila," *Archaeological Survey of India, Annual Report 1935–1936,* pp. 33–35, Pls. ix-xi; "Excavations at Taxila," *Archaeological Survey of India, Annual Report 1936–1937,* pp. 36–39, Pl. v.

[9] CBETA, T. 22, no. 1425, p. 498, a6-18.

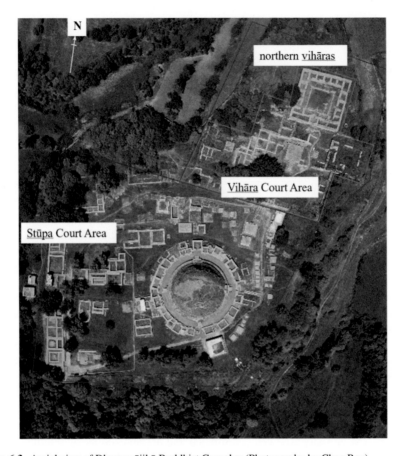

Fig. 6.3 Aerial view of Dharmarājikā Buddhist Complex (Photography by Chao Ren)

There is another square-shaped architectural ruin broken by a vihāra court, the former one being another early Buddhist early architecture yet to be researched.[10]

Jauliāñ Buddhist Complex consists of a stūpa court a vihāra court. The vihāra court lies in the east, occupying more than half of the whole site while the stūpa court in the west was divided into two parts by two platforms of different height (Figs. 6.7 and 6.8).

Main stūpa stands in the center of the southern higher part and the lower northern part was linked to vihāra in the west. There exist many votive stūpas and Buddhist shrines built almost in line around the stūpa. The vihāra court in the west is a two-story architecture with open square courtyard, central pool, drainage culverts, indoor lamp shrines, slate roads and steps. Infrastructures such as ordination hall, dining

---

[10] This information was kindly provided Professor Li Chongfeng from School of Archaeology and Museology, Peking University.

Fig. 6.4 Remnants of early railings around Dharmarajīka Stūpa (Photography by Xiao Li)

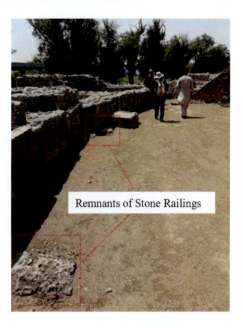

Fig. 6.5 Stairways from the ground to the outward platforms and circular pedestal of Dharmarajīka Stūpa (Photography by LiXiao)

hall, kitchen, warehouse and toilet were well-equipped, though not built together at the same time.[11]

---

[11] F. H. Wilcher, *Report on the Exploration of the Buddhist Ruins at Takht-i-Bai, January to April 1871, Punjab Government Gazette, Supplement 6th August 1874*, pp. 528–532. (Reproduced in:

Fig. 6.6 Central courtyard and pool in the northern monastery of Dharmarajīka (Photography by Xiao Li)

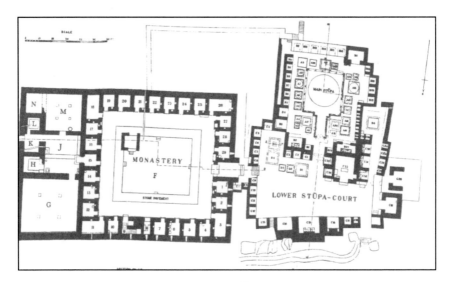

Fig. 6.7 Site plan of the Jauliāñ Buddhist Complex[12]

E. Errington, *The Western Discovery of the Art of Gandhara and the Finds of Jarmālgarhī*, Ph.D. Thesis, University of London, 1987, pp. 434–437.); J. Marshall et al., "Excavations at Taxila: The Stūpas and Monastery at Jauliāñ," *Memoirs of the Archaeological Survey of India*, No. 7, Calcutta: Superintendent Government Printing, 1921; J. Marshall, *Taxila: An Illustrated Account of Archaeological Excavations carried out at Taxila under the orders of the Government of India between the years 1913 and 1934*, Vol. 1, Cambridge: Cambridge University Press, 1951, pp. 368–388.

[12] J. Marshall, *A Guide to Taxila*, Cambridge: Cambridge University Press, 1960, Pl. XXV.

Fig. 6.8 Stairways of the main Stūpa and votive Stūpas and shrines around (Photography by LiangJian)

Takht-i-Bāhī Buddhist complex is located in the center of Gandhāra area with the architectures spreading on three spurs, stretching east–west for about 1.5 km. The most important architectural legacy lies in the central spur (Fig. 6.9). The Buddhist complex has undergone several enlargements (Fig. 6.10) and can be dated back to first century A.D., continuing to function until seventh century A.D.[13]

The main entrance of the whole complex lies in the east. The main entrance of the site seems to be on the west wall. Walking along the valley from north to south through the entrance, turning eastwards, one can finally arrive at the central court (Fig. 6.10). Between the middle stūpa court and vihāra court is the lower central court with densely-distributed votive stūpas of various patterns, which were built along with the main stūpa in the earliest phase of the complex. The south stūpa court and vihāra court were later built toward the main stūpa court, both in square and with shrines and vihāras along three sides of the building. In the southeast corner of the vihāra court is a pool, beside which are several larger rooms possibly serving as kitchen, dining hall and washroom.

The third phase of Takht-i-Bāhī from fourth to fifth century A.D. witnessed the construction of the Buddhist shrines, including the ones in the north and south of

---

[13] D. B. Spooner, "Excavations at Takht-i-Bāhī," *Archaeological Survey of India Annual Report 1907–08*, Calcutta, 1911, pp. 132–148; A. Stein, "Conservation at Takht-i-Bahi," *Archaeological Survey of India Frontier Circle 1911–1912*, 1912, Peshawar, pp. 2–3; H. Hargreaves, "Excavations at Takht-i-Bāhī," *Archaeological Survey of India Annual Report 1910–11*, Calcutta, 1914, pp. 33–39; M. H. K. Khattak, "Fresh Research on the Buddhist Monastic Complex of Takht-i-Bāhī," in P. Stewart and W. Rienjang eds., *Geography of Gandhāran Art: Proceedings of the Second International Workshop of the Gandhāra Connection Project, University of Oxford, 22nd–23rd March, 2018*, Oxford: Archaeopress, 2019, pp. 71–80.

Fig. 6.9 Aerial View of Takht-i-Bāhī Buddhist Complex (Photography by Chao Ren)

middle court yard all opening toward the central court and the ones leading to the entrance of the main stūpa court. After the three court were completed, colossal shrines, high and narrow are most likely to be equipped with monumental Buddha statue inside (Fig. 6.11). Spaces for public use like the assembly hall and the so-called basement, which are actually rooms in lower height, were added to the west of the three court in the last phase of the complex at around fifth century. A north–south brick-paved road stretched throughout the central court, linking the higher stūpa court and vihāra court.

6.3 Layouts of Buddhist Monasteries in Central Asia Area

Shortly before the Christian era, Buddhism was introduced into Tranxosiana (Area between Amu and Syr Darya) from Gandhāra in the South. There, Rouzhi ("月氏") people first became Buddhists during their settlement from nomadic life. Then Buddhism was widespread under the reign of Kushan empire when some early Buddhist monasteries began to appear in northern Bactria and Merv (ancient Margiana) (Fig. 6.12).

By fifth century A.D. when Hephthalites came to power, Buddhism, as that of the Gandhāra area, underwent a much slower development.[14] In mid-sixth century A.D., Turkic people turned to rule here. Even though they themselves were not Buddhists,

---

[14] YuTaishan, *Studies on History of Yanda* (in Chinese), Beijing: Qilu Book Company, 1986. 148.

Fig. 6.10 Site plan of Takht-i-Bāhī Buddhist Monastery (Central Spur)[15]

it was under their rule that Buddhism saw its great recovery.[16] The second phase of Buddhism popularity started at mid-seventh century A.D. when Tang dynasty controlled this region via the Anxi Frontier Command (Anxi Duhu Fu, "安西都护府") and built a certain number of Buddhist monasteries specially in Chu River valley, including the official ones like Dayun Temple (Dayun Si, "大云寺").[17] After

---

[15] Kurt A. Behrendt, *The Art of Gandhara in the Metropolitan Museum of Art*, New York: Metropolitan Museum of Art; New Haven and London: Yale University Press, 2007, p. 64, Fig. 27.

[16] Hans-J. Klimkeit, "Buddhism in Turkish Central Asia", Numen, Vol. 37, no. 1, 1990, pp. 53–69.

[17] Nuerlan Kenjiahamaiti, *Suiye* (in Chinese), Shanghai: Shanghai Guji Publishing House, 2007, pp. 78–81. For the most recent excavations by Russia and China unveiled another two Buddhist monasteries. See A. I. Torgoev et al., "A Newly Discovered Buddhist Monument in the Chu Valley

Fig. 6.11 Vihāra court with additional rooms (Photography by Chao Ren)

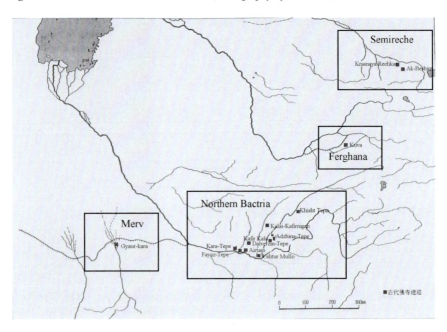

Fig. 6.12 Map of distribution of ancient Buddhist sites in Northern Central Asia (Drawn by Jiang Yonghang and LiaoZhitang)

eighth century A.D., with the expansion of Islamic culture, Buddhism was eventually extinct in Central Asia.

Following part focuses on the typical and chronologically early sites around Termez in Uzbekistan, Vakhsh valley in Tajikistan and Merv in Turkmenistan.

Kara Tepe Buddhist complex, consisting of both ground monasteries and caves, stands in the northwest of the old Termez which was initially built during Kushan period. Ever since its discovery in 1920s, it has provided us with many Buddhist architectures mainly congregating on three hills, the northern hill, the western hill and the southern hill (Fig. 6.13).These Buddhist architectures were built mostly between first and third century A.D. and declined at the end of fourth century A.D.[18]

Two types of layouts can be seen at present in Kara Tepe. The first one, also the most obvious one, is the Gandhāran type in North Hill, where a stūpa court and a vihāra court were built almost in the same line. Yet, like many other Buddhist monasteries in Gandhāra, the main stūpa in North Hill was not built to face the entrance of the vihāra part. Meanwhile, much fewer votive stūpas were built here.

The second type is the Indian type considering the Buddhist cave part widely found in West Hill and South Hill (Fig. 6.14). This reminds us of the layouts of Indian Buddhist caves in Deccan plateau. More specifically, the cave parts here can be further divided into two categories, the long and single one in west hill and the square one that can provide path for circumambulation. The latter one can be regarded as the cave presentation of the "囗"shape temple which originated in Bactria and further influence the Buddhist monasteries in Central Asia and western regions.[19]

Buddhist sites of Tajikistan are located mainly in its southwestern part and Ajina Tepe located in the Vakhsh Valley to the south of Dushanbe is still the most well-preserved one. Ajina Tepe was built and used between late seventh century A.D. and early eighth century A.D. By then, Tang dynasty has already established administrative offices in Central Asia and tried to promote Buddhism here.

Ajina Tepe Buddhist monastery consists of two courtyards (Fig. 6.15). It was constructed in a special way that buildings with roof such as houses and corridors were built from the underground, creating "cellar holes," and therefore, the surrounding wall of whole complex is irregularly rectangle (Fig. 6.16). In the south is a vihāra

---

(Northern Kyrgyzstan)," translated by Ntalia Magnes, in *Reports of the State Hermitage Museum* LXX, 2013, pp. 193–202: The Shanxi Academy of Archaeology and Ethnology of National Academy of Sciences of the Republic of Kyrgyztan, "Preliminary Reports of the excavation of the western part of the Rechka site in Kyrgyzstan 2018–2019" (in Chinese), *Kaogu yu Wenwu*, 2020, Vol. 3, pp. 37–51.

[18] G. Fussman, *Monuments bouddhiques de Termez = Termez buddhist monuments: catalogue des inscriptions sur poteries*, I, 2, Paris: Edition-Diffusion de Boccard, 2011, pp. 272–264.

[19] Б. А. Литвинскийи, Т. И. Зеймаль: *Аджина-тепе: Архитектура, Живопись, Скульптура*, 1971, М.: Искусство, 1971, С. 145; H. G. Franz, Von Gandhara bis Pagan: Kultbauten des Buddhismus und Hinguismus in Süd-und Zentralasien, Granz-Austria: Akademische Drucku, Verlagsanstalt, 1979,pp. 14–60; B. J. Stavisky, "On the Formation of Two Types of Buddhist Temples in Central Asia," in *Orient und Okzident im Spiegel der Kunst: Festschrift Heinrich Gerhard Franz zum 70 Geburtstag*, Graz-Austria: Akademische Druck-und Verlagsanstalt, 1986, pp. 381–388. For study on "囗"shape Buddhist temple in western regions, see Xiaolu Chen, A Study on the origin of Buddhist Temples in the Western Regions (in Chinese), Kaogu, 2010, Vol. 11, pp. 79–90.

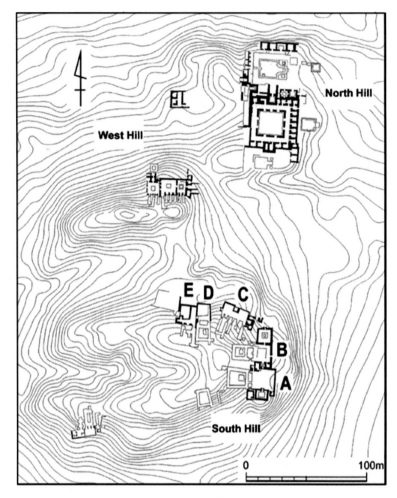

Fig. 6.13 Site plan of Kara Tepe Buddhist Complex[20]

court with a central open yard and some rooms outside such as and pillared gathering hall and central shrine opposed to the entrance, with three statue pedestals along the inner wall and a brick-paved path leading to the north court. Larger than the south one, the north court was designed as a stūpa court. The stūpa base is of multi-story corbel structure yet the stūpa body was already broken, with stairways in four directions and votive stūpas of similar type of the main stūpa. Extending from the central yard is corridor rooms which can be divided into four parts. In Eastern part of the corridor lies a monumental 12-m-long reclining Buddha nirvāṇa statue.

---

[20] G. Fussman, *Monuments bouddhiques de Termez = Termez buddhist monuments: catalogue des inscriptions sur poteries*, I, 2, Paris: Edition-Diffusion de Boccard, pp. 159, Planche 21.

Fig. 6.14 Entrance of the Buddhist Cave in Kara Tepe A complex in South Hill (photography by LiuZhijia)

6.4 Comparison of Buddhist Architectural Elements of Gandhāra Area, Central Asia and Western Regions

Cultural communication in history was actually less convenient between ancient Xinjiang and Gandhāra area, as they were adjacent to each other yet divided by formidable plateau. With a much younger history than that of Gandhārā, Buddhism along the northern border of Tarim basin, in particular, as seen from the surviving Buddhist monasteries, received more influence form Central Asia than from Gandhāra area.

Overall, when Buddhist Art of architecture first entered Tarim basin in Xinjiang, it carried plenty of elements from Transoxiana and Central Asia. However, local traditions of western regions and central plain elements played an increasingly important role. While Buddhism of Gandhāra and Central Asia turned to decline for Islamization, Buddhist monasteries in western regions, on the other hand, continued developing its own characteristic under the impact of Buddhist culture from ancient China for long time afterwards (Fig. 6.17).

Due to space limitation, this part only involves Buddhist sites of similar style to those in Gandhāra–Central Asia and comparison among them.

Fig. 6.15 Site plan of Ajina Tepe Buddhist Complex[21]

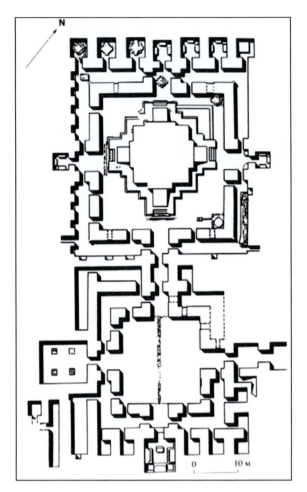

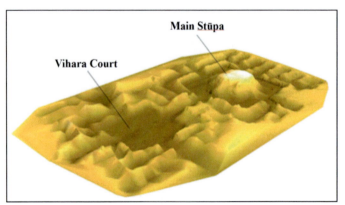

Fig. 6.16 Reconstruction of Ajina Tepe[22]

6 A Comparative Study of Layouts of Buddhist Monasteries in Gandhāra … 103

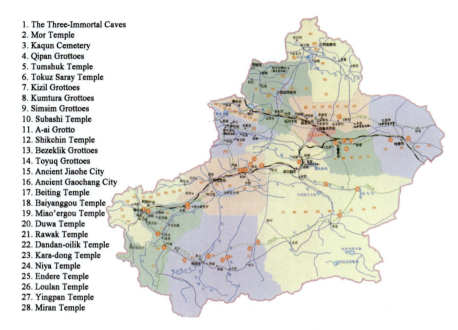

1. The Three-Immortal Caves
2. Mor Temple
3. Kaqun Cemetery
4. Qipan Grottoes
5. Tumshuk Temple
6. Tokuz Saray Temple
7. Kizil Grottoes
8. Kumtura Grottoes
9. Simsim Grottoes
10. Subashi Temple
11. A-ai Grotto
12. Shikchin Temple
13. Bezeklik Grottoes
14. Toyuq Grottoes
15. Ancient Jiaohe City
16. Ancient Gaochang City
17. Beiting Temple
18. Baiyanggou Temple
19. Miao'ergou Temple
20. Duwa Temple
21. Rawak Temple
22. Dandan-oilik Temple
23. Kara-dong Temple
24. Niya Temple
25. Endere Temple
26. Loulan Temple
27. Yingpan Temple
28. Miran Temple

Fig. 6.17 Map of distribution of ancient Buddhist sites in Xinjiang[23]

First is the comparison among layouts of stūpa, Dharmarajika Stūpa in Pakistan, Zurmala Stūpa in Uzbekistan,[24] Mo'er Buddhist monastery of Kashgar[25] (Fig. 6.18), Eastern Part of Subash Buddhist Temple (Dongsi, "东寺") of Kucha (Fig. 6.19) and Rawak Buddhist monastery of Khotan in Xinjiang today (Fig. 6.20) as examples.

From the layout of the Dharmarājīka Stūpa in Taxila, Pakistan, we can see the basic layout of the stūpa exchanging from a low circle pedestal one to a square pedestal one which soon became fixed as the square pedestal occupied an increasingly large part of the whole stūpa, from less than half to nearly two-third as seen in Zurmala

---

[21] V. Fominikh, "The Buddhist Monuments of Adjina-tepa", *The Silk Road*, 6/1, 2008, pp. 38–44, Fig. 2.

[22] 加藤九祚: <中央アジア北部仏教遺跡の研究>, 奈良: シルクロード学研究センター, 1997, p. 28.

[23] Huo Xuchu and QiXiaoshan, *The Buddhist Art in Xinjiang Along the Silk Road* (in Chinese), Urumqi: Xinjiang University Press, 2006, p. 5.

[24] A. Ulmasov, *Reconstruction of the Zurmala Buddhist Stūpa in Termez, Uzbekistan*, International Journal of Innovative Science, Engineering and Technology (I-JISET), 2018, Vol. 5, Issue 5, pp. 93, 95–96; A. Iwamoto, "A Study on the Prosperity and Decline of Buddhist Sites in Northern Bactria: Kara Tepe and Zurmala," *The Rissho international journal of academic research in culture and society*, 2, 2019, pp. 151–178.

[25] For most Recent excavation report on Mo'er Buddhist monastery Site from 2019 to 2021, see XiaoXiaoyong, Shi Haocheng and ZengXu, "New Discoveries of the Archaeological Excavation in the Mo'er Temple Site in Kashgar," Xinjiang 2019–2021 (in Chinese), *Xiyu Yanjiu*, 2022, Vol. 1, pp. 66–73.

Fig. 6.18 Side view and aerial view of Mo'er Buddhist Monastery in Kashgar. (Photography by Li Xiao)

stūpa. Special attention should by paid to the pedestal of stūpa of Rawak site that comprises almost half of the whole stūpa body, which resembles the Dharmarājīka Stūpa. This may be due to the introduction of Buddhism into southern Tarim Basin from Gandhāra area through Kashmir.

Second is the functional change of yard and pool in Buddhist Monastery. Buddhism was born in South Asia subcontinent where climate is timid and scorching, and it was important for monks to clear summer-heat and purify their body. Therefore, in the center of the vihāra court circled by vihāras, there was usually, if not a pillared hall, a spacious open yard with a central stone-made pool for bathing and cooling.

When Buddhism came to Central Asia where days are less scorching than in India, bathing became an unnecessary rite. Moreover, the climate is so dry with local shortage of water resources and strong evaporation, that water in the pool would have dried up or gone bad quickly. Most importantly, stones for building a pool as in Gandhāra are in scarcity in Central Asia while local loess can hardly prevent pool water from leaking. Under this circumstance, pool made of loess still exists in vihāra court in Central Asia yet in a shallower form as something for decoration and as

Fig. 6.19 Side view and aerial view of Subashi Buddhist Monastery in Kucha. (Photography by LiXiao)

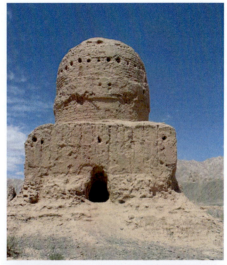

places for gathering, such as the pool within Fayaz Tepe in Termez, Uzbekistan[26] (Fig. 6.21).

As Buddhism entered Tarim Basin of extreme dryness, bathing became extravagant. Yet since architectural elements of a monastery were already established in Buddhist scriptures (especially vinava) and construction traditions, the pool was transformed into a well supplying water here. For example, there used to be two wells in the yard of Buddhist monastery E-27 (Dafosi, "大佛寺") in Ancient Jiaohe City Ruins(Jiaohe Gucheng, "交河故城"), of which only one well was truly made for drawing water, the other modelled in a well-shape yet without actual function[27] (Fig. 6.22).

---

[26] T. K. ムクルティチェフ著, 川崎建三訳: <最近の調査研究による北バクトリアの仏教僧院址ファヤズテパ>, 2016年, *Silk Road Studies*, No. 9, pp. 15–25.

[27] LiXiao, *Jiaohe Gucheng de Xingzhi Buju (in Chinese)*, Beijing: Cultural Relic Press, pp. 109–112.

Fig. 6.20 Side view and aerial view of Rawak Buddhist Monastery of Khotan. (Photography by Qi Xiaoshan and Chen Fan)

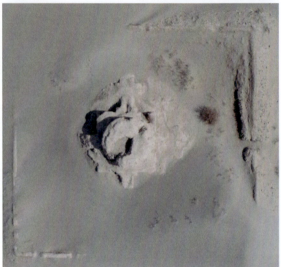

6.5 Conclusion

Buddhist monasteries, as the most realistic and direct evidence and reflection of historic development of Buddhism, had undergone great changes since its origination in India. Generally speaking, changes of layout of Buddhist monasteries from Gandhāra Area to Central Asia and Tarim Basin is a complicated process of different regional cultures and also a vivid reflection of distinct social structure and belief swift in terms of architectural structure. After such initial form as ārāmas in Buddha's lifetime, representative stūpa-court cum vihāra court configuration in Gandhāra appeared around first century A.D. and "▢"shape Buddhist temple was created first in Northern Central Asia that further influenced most of the Buddhist monasteries in Tarim Basin. The layouts development of Buddhist monasteries shows an obvious tendency of becoming more organized in zone division and more exclusive from outside world. From the high walls and small doors, we can understand the intensification of religious discipline and social authorization, mirroring inner

6 A Comparative Study of Layouts of Buddhist Monasteries in Gandhāra …

Fig. 6.21 Loess pool in Vihāra court of Fayaz Tepe in Termez, Uzbekistan. (Photography by LiXiao)

Fig. 6.22 Real and fake wells within Buddhist monastery E-27 in Ancient Jiaohe City Ruins of Turfan, Xinjiang

conflicts of the society at various stages in history of Buddhism. Various functions were gradually integrated into one single unit. That is a say, worship area and dwelling area all into one, indicates the worldly tendency of Buddhism under the patronage of both the saṅgha and the laity, which were always the two most dominative driving force for the developments of Buddhist monasteries since Buddhism's birth in India.

Bibliography

Behrendt KA (2007) The Art of Gandhara in the Metropolitan Museum of Art. Metropolitan Museum of Art, New York; Yale University Press, New Haven and London

Education Department of State Administration of Cultural Heritagee (1993) Summary of Archaeologyof Buddhist Grottoes (in Chinese). CulturalRelics Press, Beijing

Fominikh V (2008) The Buddhist monuments of Adjina-tepa. The Silk Road 6(1):38–44

Franz HG (1979) Von Gandhara bis Pagan: Kultbauten des Buddhismus und Hinguismus in Süd-und Zentralasien. Akademische Drucku, Verlagsanstalt, Granz-Austria

Fussman G (2011) Monuments bouddhiques de Termez= Termez buddhist monuments: catalogue des inscriptions sur poteries, I, 2. Edition-Diffusion de Boccard, Paris

Hargreaves H (1914) Excavations at Takht-i-Bāhī. Archaeological Survey of India Annual Report 1910–11, Calcutta, pp 33–39

Iwamoto A (2019) A study on the prosperity and decline of Buddhist sites in Northern Bactria: Kara Tepe and Zurmala. The Rissho Int J Acad Res Cult Soc 2:151–178

Kenjiahamaiti N (2007) Suiye (in Chinese). Shanghai Guji Publishing House, Shanghai

Khan S, Siddiqi AD. Excavations at Taxila. Archaeological Survey of India, Annual Report 1935–1936, pp 33–35

Khan S, Siddiqi AD. Excavations at Taxila. Archaeological Survey of India, Annual Report 1934–1935, pp 28–31

Khan S, Siddiqi AD. Excavations at Taxila. Archaeological Survey of India, Annual Report 1936–1937, pp 36–39

Khattak MHK (2018) Fresh research on the Buddhist Monastic Complex of Takht-i-Bāhī. In: Stewart P, Rienjang W (eds) Geography of Gandhāran Art: Proceedings of the Second International Workshop of the Gandhāra Connection Project, University of Oxford, 22nd – 23rd March, 2018. Archaeopress, Oxford, pp 71–80

Klimkeit H-J (1990) Buddhism in Turkish Central Asia. Numen 37(1):53–69

Kuwayama S (2006) Pilgrimage route changes and the decline of Gandhāra. In: Brancaccio P, Behrendt KA (eds) Gandhāran Buddhism. UBC Press, Vancouver

Marshall J et al (1921) Excavations at Taxila: The Stupas and Monastery at Jauliāñ. In: Memoirs of the archaeological survey of India, No. 7. Superintendent Government Printing, Calcutta

Marshall J (1951) Taxila: an illustrated account of archaeological excavations carried out at Taxila under the orders of the Government of India between the years 1913 and 1934, vol 1. Cambridge University Press, Cambridge

Marshall J (1960) A guide to Taxila. Cambridge University Press, Cambridge

Rienjang W, Stewart P (eds) (2019) The geography of Gandhāran Art: proceedings of the second international workshop of the Gandhāra connections project

Salmon R (1999) Ancient Buddhist scrolls from Gandhāra: The British Library Kharoṣṭhī Fragments. University of Washington Press, Seattle

Sarkar H (1966) Studies in early Buddhist architecture of India. Oriental Publishers, New Delhi

Spooner DB (1911) Excavations at Takht-i-Bāhī. Archaeological Survey of India Annual Report 1907–08, Calcutta, pp 132–148

Stavisky BJ (1986) On the formation of two types of Buddhist temples in Central Asia. In: Orient und Okzident im Spiegel der Kunst: Festschrift Heinrich Gerhard Franz zum 70 Geburtstag. Akademische Druck-und Verlagsanstalt, Graz-Austria, pp 381–388

Stein A (1912) Conservation at Takht-i-Bahi. Archaeological Survey of India Frontier Circle 1911–1912, Peshawar, pp 2–3

T=大正新脩大藏經 (Taisho Tripitaka) (Accordingto CBETA)

Taishan Y (1986) Studies on History of Yanda (in Chinese). Qilu Book Company, Beijing

The Shanxi Academy of Archaeology and Ethnology of National Academy of Sciences of the Republic of Kyrgyztan (2020) Preliminary reports of the excavation of the western part of the Rechka site in Kyrgyzstan 2018–2019 (in Chinese). Kaogu yu Wenwu 3:37–51

Torgoev AI et al (2013) A newly discovered Buddhist Monument in the Chu Valley (Northern Kyrgyzstan). Tanslated by Magnes N, Reports of the State Hermitage Museum LXX, pp 193–202

Ulmasov A (2018) Reconstruction of the Zurmala Buddhist Stupa in Termez, Uzbekistan. Int J Innov Sci Eng Tachnol (I-JISET) 5(5):93, 95–96

Wilcher FH (1874) Report on the exploration of the Buddhist Ruins at Takht-i-Bai, January to April 1871, Punjab Government Gazette, Supplement 6th August 1874, pp 528–532. (Reproduced in: Errington E (1987) The Western Discovery of the Art of Gandhara and the Finds of Jarmālgarhī, PhD Thesis, University of London, pp 434–437)

Xiao L (2013) Jiaohe Gucheng de Xingzhi Buju. Cultural Relic Press, Beijing

Xiaolu C (2010) A study on the origin of Buddhist temples in the Western Regions (in Chinese). Kaogu 11:79–90

Xiaoyong X, Shi H, Zeng X (2022) New discoveries of the archaeological excavation in the MO'er temple site in Kashgar, Xinjiang 2019–2021(in Chinese). Xiyu Yanjiu 1:66–73

Xuchu H, Xiaoshan Q (2006) The Buddhist Art in Xinjiang along the silk road (in Chinese). Xinjiang University Press, Urumqi

Yungang Academy, Shanxi Provincial Institute of Archaeology and Datong Municipal Institute of Archaeology (2021) Excavation Report of Buddhist Temple ruins at Hilltop of Yungang Grottoes (in Chinese), I-III. Cultural Relics Press Beijing

Литвинскийи БА, Зеймаль ТИ (1971) Аджина-тепе: Архитектура, Живопись, Скульптура, М.: Искусство

加藤九祚: <中央アジア北部仏教遺跡の研究>, 奈良: シルクロード学研究センター, 1997.

T.K. ムクルティチェフ著, 川崎建三訳: <最近の調査研究による北バクトリアの仏教僧院址ファヤズテパ>, Silk Road Studies, No. 9, 2016年, pp 15–25

Chapter 7
PIXE Analysis of Glazed Ceramics of the Early Islamic Period at Hazara University Museum Collection

Shakirullah, Muhammad Zahoor, Ihsanullah Jan, and Abdul Basit

Abstract The study of ancient ceramics provides valuable information about different aspects of past human behavior such as their trade and commerce, their rituals, technologies as well as exploitation of the resources. Particle-induced X-ray emission (PIXE) is a non-destructive analysis method used to study the thin decorative coating of antique ceramics. 15 glazed fragments of Early Islamic Ceramics from Hazara University Museum, Hazara University Mansehra, and Pakistan were studied. We used Particle-induced X-ray emission spectroscopy (PIXE) to investigate the metallic minerals in the pigments of glazed ceramics. The aim of the study was to identify metals of mineral pigments from the Islamic Period ceramics and concludes about the culture and civilization of the cited era.

Keywords Archeological science · Glazed ceramics · Spectroscopy

7.1 Introduction

The introduction of glazed pottery is also attributed to the Ghaznavid. The glazed ceramics are famous due to its distinctive features and are exhibited in different museums of the world. The Hazara University Museum also exhibits a peculiar collection of glazed ceramics, which were donated by Eng. Awais Ahmad Ghani, the former Governor of Khyber Pakhtunkhwa. The present study focuses on the classification and analysis of the said collection. This glazed collection reflects that the people of that particular period were highly skilled in the art of geometric, floral, zoomorphic, anthropomorphic and calligraphic ornamentation. These motifs were used for the decoration purposes. Right from the beginning, the Muslim

---

Shakirullah (✉) · M. Zahoor · I. Jan
Department of Archaeology, Hazara University, Mansehra 21300, Pakistan
e-mail: shakir@hu.edu.pk

A. Basit
Taxila Institute of Asian Civilizations, Quid-I-Azam University, Islamabad, Pakistan

© SDX Joint Publishing 2023
X. Li (ed.), *Major Archaeological Discoveries Along the Chinese Silk Road*,
Silk Road Research Series, https://doi.org/10.1007/978-981-99-0659-8_8

artists have used plant motifs and patterns, portraying natural as well as stylized variety. Potter and artists drew inspiration from different types of plants and flowers at different times. Different patterns were created, using a range of techniques, including repetition of a motif within various grids, reflective and rotational symmetry, and freehand designs. During the early phase, the craftsmen continued the former semi-naturalisticmotifs, inherited from Byzantine, Coptic and Sasanian.

The pottery found in Bust and Lashkar-i- Bazar was the object of a systematic study by the archeologist Jean-Claude Gardin, who classified all the finds into different categories. A first subdivision concerned the separation between glazed and unglazed pottery. Unglazed pottery forms a relatively homogeneous set as far as paste features are concerned, and was further subdivided into five groups and then in series, depending on form and decoration. As for glazed pottery, Gardin operated a subdivision into three major types, also related to chronology; these types were characterized, respectively, by painted decoration on engobe, painted and incised decoration on engobe and painted decoration without engobe.

7.2 Background

The Samanids appeared as one of the provincial dynasties under the Abbasids in the region now eastern Iran and Uzbekistan during last decades of the ninth century A.D. under whom, Khurasan and Transoxiana, the historical region of Central Asia and Iran developed. Samarqand, Bukhara, Balkh, Nishapur and Merve were their major centers of Samanids (Negmatov 1983: 84) as shown in Fig. 7.1. In 977, Subuktagin the founder of Ghaznavid dynasty and commandant of Samanids ruled on the large parts of Iran, Afghanistan, much of Transoxiana and the northwest Indian subcontinent from 977 to 1186 A.D. (Bosworth 1983: 104). Mahmud, the son and successor of Subuktagin brought the entire Afghanistan and the former Samanid areas to the south of Oxus, under his rule and laid the proper foundation of the Ghaznavid realm (Bosworth 1983: 104). Soon he extended his empire from Azerbaijan to Ganges Valley (west to east) and from Khwarzam and northern Oxus region to the Sind and Makran—the modern Pakistan (North to south). Since then Ghazna remained as a pivot of the learning, arts and crafts, and culture in the region till the thirteenth century (Bosworth 1983: 107). Following the same tradition, the Ghaznavids, in particular, and the subsequent dynasties in general were the patrons of art and culture at numerous major centers of the region. The Masud's successors could not hold such a vast empire, eventually lost the Ghazna to the Ghorids and were confined to the eastern most part of their empire—the present-day Pakistan until they were also completely overrun by the Ghorids. The territories of Afghanistan then came under the Mongols.

Ghazna and Laskhari Bazar, the two capitals of the Ghaznavids have been inspected by various missions like the IsMEO Italian Archeological Mission (from 1957 to 1966) and the Frenchs' excavations of Lashkari Bazar. During the course of the later investigations at Masud's palace a variety of ceramics have been unearthed,

7 PIXE Analysis of Glazed Ceramics of the Early Islamic Period at Hazara …

Fig. 7.1 Ghaznavid Empire at its greatest extent (Boyle 1968)

while at Bust, pottery kilns have been exposed (Gardin 1963). Gardin has studied these ceramics systematically (Gardin 1963).

However, the pottery of these particular regions has been subjected to chemical analysis by French scholar Jacques Boissier (1963) and later on by the Italians (Gulmini et al. 2013).

The present paper is the result of the primary scientific examination of a set of glazed fragments, displayed at Hazara Archeological and Ethnological Museum Hazara University Mansehra KP, Pakistan. The fragments were in private collection and donated to the Hazara University's Museum by the former Governor of NWFP, modern the Khyber Pakhtunkhwa Province of Pakistan. The origin of the fragments linked to ancient Bust and Lashkar-i Bazar, southern Afghanistan. All the fragments are characterized by highly calcareous bodies, and all of them coated with a transparent lead glaze.

7.3 Particle-Induced X-Ray Emission (PIXE) a Non-destructive Analytical Method

Particle-induced X-ray emission (PIXE) a non-destructive analysis method adapted to the thin decorative coating of antique ceramics (Leon 2012). The technique is used to determine the bulk elemental composition of artifacts due to its fast and simultaneously ability to measure a large number of elements with good accuracy and without any damage to the sample. The decrease of protons energy from 3 meV (standard condition) to 1–5 meV provide limitation for the analysis depth to the coating thickness without significant alteration of the results (Leon 2012). When charged particles pass through matter, X-ray is emitted. Each element has specific spectral identity, which is link to their concentrations. It is used for elemental studies (Sc 1989).

Micro-PIXE is an essential technique for the non-destructive analysis of paintings and antiques. It provides only an elemental analysis, it can be used to differentiate and measure layers within the thickness of an artifact's coating. The PIXE technique is advantageous as it does not need laborious work up during sample preparation. There are various factors, which influence the concentration of elements in the artifacts. These include firing process, the use of pottery and interaction of soil with the material of the clay (Z. Elekes).

It has low background radiation, good sensitivity for light elements and lower secondary excitation in thick targets and sensitive toward the detection of light element (Miranda 1996). PIXE is as non-destructive technique and cannot damage or alter the inherited nature of artifacts. Through scientific methods history of migration process, cultural characteristics and in objectives manner preservation and conservation of cultural heritage can be revealed (Tabacniks and Hunt 2016).

7.4 Use of PIXE in Pottery

The differences in pottery formation could indicate different techniques of preparing clay.

Elemental analysis is difficult in the case of archeological artifacts because the material are strongly heterogeneous and contain wide range of composition although apparently similar materials (Johansson and Campbell). PIXE analysis can determine the primary composition and minor elemental patterns of clay fabrics, which is beneficial in decoding trade links between ancient nations (Fleming 1992).

7.5 Materials and Methods

Fifteen glazed sherds from the Islamic Period were studied (Fig. 7.3). The shreds were reported from Hazara cultural and Ethnological Museum Hazara University, Mansehra Khyber Pakhtunkhwa, Pakistan. The museum is under the Department of Archeology Hazara University Mansehra and exhibits a rich collection of glazed ceramics of the Ghaznavid period which were donated by Eng. Awais Ahmed Ghani, the former Governor of Khyber Pakhtunkhwa province of Pakistan. These glazed

7 PIXE Analysis of Glazed Ceramics of the Early Islamic Period at Hazara … 115

ceramics are famous due to its distinctive features that show the people of that particular period were highly skilled in the art of geometric, floral, zoomorphic, anthropomorphic and calligraphic ornamentation. The following selected shreds Fig. 7.2 for present study are well preserved and displayed at the museum.

Fig. 7.2 Ghaznavid glaze Ceramic at Hazara University's Museum

Fig. 7.3 Examples of analyzed glazed sherds of Early Islamic Period

The PIXE analysis, which is 100 times more sensitive than EDS and its sensitivity is 0.1 ppm, was performed at the National Centre for Physics, Islamabad.

PIXE experiment was carried out using KBr pellet (13 mm die) pellets. Along with samples, standards and RMs were used in the experiment. The characteristic X-rays of the elements present in all the samples were measured using a Si (Li) detector with a resolution of 160 eV at 5.9 keV. A PC-based multi-channel analyzer, calibrated with 55Fe X-ray source, was used. Charge normalized count rate from the targets were used for concentration calculation.

7.6 Result and Discussion

The PIXE analyses were performed using two X-ray detectors, one for major elements and one for trace elements. The PIXI results presented in Fig. 7.1 show elements concentration calculated from the each selected samples. It was found that in the sample A, the aluminum (Al), sulfur (S), and potassium (K) were most dominant element with concentration up to 3500 ppm. The terraces of calcium (Ca) also been detected in this sample.

In the sample B, the graph of Al, S, and K was higher among rest of the elements detected with minor concentration. Similarly, the samples C and D showed the same result with Al, S, and K as dominant elements. The highest graphs of Al, S, and K have been detected in the sample E with almost 6000 ppm concentration. The samples G, H, I, and J have almost the same ppm concentration of Al, S, and K detected between 4000 and 3000 ranges with some other elements. The sample H and I also showed enough concentration of repeated elements Al, S, and K, but in sample G, the graph of repeated elements could be seen in lower position as shown in Fig. 7.4.

In the sample J, the element Ca was detected with highest ppm concentration. In the sample K, only the KK found with large amount and rest of the elements, i.e., Al and Ca were present in minor basis. The sample L showed ppm concentration of Al with its peak with small amount of Ca. In the sample M, Al, S, and K were the most dominant elements with enough ppm concentration after Ca. Similarly, in the sample N, enough ppm concentration of potassium (K) has been detected, and the sample O showed Al, S, and K as dominant elements. The other elements, i.e., Ti, V, Cr, Mn, Fe, Cu, Zn, Hg, Au, and Bi also been detected with minor ppm concentration in all the samples as shown in Fig. 7.4.

7.7 Discussion

Analytical data of PIXE (Table 7.1) shows that the pigments are mainly consisted of aluminum (Al), sulfur (S), potassium (K), calcium (Ca), titanium (Ti), vanadium (V), chromium (Cr), Manganese (Mn), iron (Fe), copper (Cu), zinc (Zn), arsenic (As),

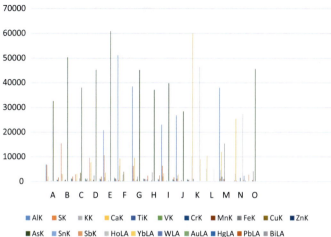

Fig. 7.4 ppm concentration of the elements of Ghaznavid glazes

gold (Au), mercury (Hg), lead (Pb), and bismuth (Bi). Mostly, the metal minerals used to obtain blue, green, yellow, red, and brown colors are identified. The main results of the present work are summarized in Tables 7.1 and 7.2. They show an evident overall stability of the compositional pattern for a given color. This seems to be independent on the particular decoration, shape, typology, and time and could be interpreted as an indication of the use of unique production technology in the past. The pigments detected in glazed ceramics can be poisonous and injurious to health which shows the glazed ceramic objects used in the past for decorative purposes only, not for daily use. The following Table 7.2 clearly shows the elements and its yielding colorant.

7.8 Conclusion

The present study aims to investigate the composition of the glaze, the temperature to which the glaze is fired and the kiln atmosphere during firing of the selected glazed ceramics. For this purpose, 15 shreds from Hazara University's Museum were analyzed using PIXE. The selected glazed shreds are dated back to Ghaznavid period. The Ghaznavid Ceramic Glazes a variety of colors show that the glazes have undergone different temperature treatments and have different compositions.

Table 7.1 ppm concentration of the elements of Ghaznavid glazes (samples A–O)

Sample	AlK	SK	KK	CaK	TiK	VK	CrK	MnK	FeK	CuK	ZnK
A	6899.9	6735.6	706.7	1989.5	66.5	8.7	8.5	19.8	308.4	690e-3	1.6
B	0	15,458.6	3134.7	2882.4	71.9	22.0	43.6	545.2	788.1	32.1	3.1
C	0	2901.4	851.1	3074.8	175.5	84.3	48.5	104.4	1279.3	3518.8	23.0
D	383.6	9546.5	1074.8	7790.3	154.2	30.6	118.7	669.3	2429.8	13.0	0
E	20,898.8	10,580.0	1812.2	3531.8	100.6	10.0	68.6	42.7	512.8	8.7	0
F	51,201.7	511.3	6350.9	9311.2	255.4	8.2	31.4	355.5	2713.8	3899.9	0
G	38,539.9	6201.5	1135.9	9562.7	213.6	48.0	98.8	738.9	2006.5	23.7	16.6
H	833.5	2361.8	0	0	36.5	3.8	39	388.9	3766.7	78.9	18.8
I	23,049.3	6321.6	1976.8	3255.1	116.9	2.4	25.8	18.2	410.9	0	0
J	26,836.8	1106.0	2382.3	2906.4	175.9	30.5	31.0	130.1	598.5	19.1	13.4
K	0	0	10,081.9	59,998.5	1021.0	0	0	0	0	0	0
L	0	0	5162.4	10,358.0	0	0	112.7	0	0	0	0
M	38,013.6	1066.9	4625.4	11,983.9	1948.9	63.7	59.3	1029.5	15,448.9	108.2	88.1
N	0	438.6	3114.4	25,448.2	244.4	0	0	0	0	90.0	1548.8
O	0	2798.2	0	0	89.6	4.4	33.0	498.4	4199.3	175.8	23.3

Sample	AsK	SnK	SbK	HoLA	YbLA	WLA	AuLA	HgLA	PbLA	BiLA
A	32,584.7	0	0	0	0	0	744.9	585.8	1576.7	245.2
B	50,344.1	0	0	0	0	0	1336.7	938.0	1988.2	124.5
C	37,995.0	0	0	0	0	0	1320.3	1015.6	509.6	1305.2
D	45,264.2	0	0	0	0	0	1179.1	855.2	1964.7	434.8
E	60,903.6	0	0	0	0	0	1688.3	1234.2	1120.5	728.6

(continued)

Table 7.1 (continued)

Sample	AsK	SnK	SbK	HoLA	YbLA	WLA	AuLA	HgLA	PbLA	BiLA
F	0	0	0	0	0	0	20.8	0	0	0
G	45,252.3	0	0	0	0	0	1229.8	1014.7	1042.0	928.6
H	37,162.9	0	0	48.1	0	0	1053.6	706.4	2431.5	0
I	39,784.0	0	0	0	0	0	868.0	718.4	1656.0	352.9
J	28,420.4	0	0	0	0	0	968.3	696.2	554.8	803.3
K	0	0	0	46,441.3	9008.1	0	0	0	0	0
L	0	26.1	0	4950.4	0	0	0	0	0	5.7
M	0	0	0	13.4	0	0	16.8	0	0	0
N	0	0	30.7	27,415.6	655.6	2336.3	0	361.0	0	0
O	45,628.2	0	0	208.0	0	0	0	0	0	0

Table 7.2 Elements and its yielding colorant

Element (in the form of oxides)	Yielded color	Explanation
Chromium oxide	Chrome red	Needs lead glaze fired at cone 08 or below
	Chrome yellow	Needs lead-soda glaze fired at cone 08 or below
Chrome and zinc	Yield brown	
Chrome plus tin	Yields pink, grayed pink, and warm browns	
Cobalt oxide	Intense blue	Cobalt is an extremely powerful colorant that almost always produces an intense blue
Copper oxide	Green and red	Copper generally gives green in oxidation and red in reduction. Copper yields a lovely range of greens in lead glazes. *Copper increases lead's solubility*
Iron oxide	Light tan and straw to deep, rich browns	Iron produces warm colors ranging from light tan and straw to deep, rich browns
Gold	Pink, red and purple	
Silver and bismuth	Used in luster overglazes	

Bibliography

Anarbaev AA, Ilyasova SR (2000) Glazed ceramics of 11th century Ferghana. Ozbekiston Moddiy Madaniati Tarikhi 31:212–217

Boissier J (1963) Appendice I: Étude Chimique de la Céramique de Lashkari Bazar. In: Lashkari Bazar. Une Residence Royale Ghaznévide, II, Les Trouvailles, Céramiques et Monnaies de Lashkari Bazar et de Bust (J. C. Gardin), LibrairieC. Klincksieck, Paris

Bosworth CE (1983) "The Ghaznavids". In: Asimov MS, Bosworth CE (eds) History of civilizations of central Asia, vol. IV. UNESCO. France

Brusenko LG (1976) Ceramic craft and production at Binket. Antikvariata Tashkenti 80–114

Elekes Z (n.d.) Application of Micri-PIXE and MicroPIXE techniques in the field of archaeology

Fehérvári G, Shokoohy M (1980) Archeological Notes on Lashkari Bazar. In: Wiener Zeitschrift für die Kunde des Morgenlandes, vol 72. Published by Department of Oriental Studies, University of Vienna, pp 83–95

Fleming SJ, Swan CP (1992) Recent application of PIXE spectrometry in archaeology 11. Characterization of Chinese pottery exported to the Islamic world. In: Nuclear instruments and methods in physics research section B: beam interaction with material and atoms, pp 528–537

Gardin JC (1963) Lashkari Bazar. Une Résidence Royale Ghaznévide, II, Les Trouvailles, Céramiques et Monnaies deLashkari Bazar et de Bust. Librairie C. Klincksieck, Paris

Gulmini M, Giannini R, Lega AM, Manna G, Mirti P (2013) Technology of Production of Ghaznavid Glazed Pottery from Bust and lashkar-i Bazar (Afghanistan). Archaeometry

Henshaw CM (2010) Early Islamic Ceramics and Glazes of Akhsiket, Uzbekistan. Phd Thesis, University College London

Herrmann G, Kurbansakhotov K, Simpson J (2001) The International Merv Project preliminary report on the ninth year (2000). Iran 39:9–52
Ilyasova SR (1986) Glazed ceramics from the upper layers of Eski Akhsi. Istoria Materialnoi Kulturi Uzbekistana 20:146–153
Jenkins M (1983) Islamic pottery a brief history. The Metropolitan Museum of Art Bulletin/Spring
Johansson SA, Campbell JL (n.d.) Partical-Induced X-ray emission spectrometer (PIXE) 153
Johansson SA (1989) PIXE: a noval technique for elemental analysis. Endeavour 48–53
Khan AN (1995) Ghaznin and its environs: geographical, anthropological and historical by Major HG Raverty. Sangi Meel Publications, Lahore
Leon P (2012) Nuclear instruments and methods in physics research section B: beam interactions with material and atoms, pp 45–52
Miranda J (1996) Nuclear instruments and methods in physics research section B: beam interactions with material and atoms, pp 346–351
Mason RB (2004) Shine like the sun: lustre-painted and associated pottery from the medieval Middle East. Mazda Publishers, Costa Mesa, Calif
Negmatov NN (1983) "The Samanid State". In: Asimov MS, Bosworth CE (eds) History of civilizations of Central Asia, vol. IV, UNESCO. France
Priestley H (1999) Afghanistan and its inhabitants. Translated form the Hayat-i-Afghani by Muhammad Hayat Khan. Originally published in 1874. Lahore: Sangi Meel Publication
Shishkina GV (1979) Glazed ceramics of Sogd, Tashkent
Tabacniks MR, Hunt A (2016) Particle induced X-ray emission and its application for ceramics analysis. Archaeology methodology and techniques, scientific archaeology. The oxford Hand book of Archaeological ceramic Analysis
Watson O (2004) Ceramics from Islamic lands. Thames & Hudson in association with the al-Sabah Collection, Dar al-Athar al-Islamiyyah, Kuwait National Museum, New York

Chapter 8
Some Theoretical Issues in the Development of Prehistoric Civilizations in the Region of Xiyu

Tao Shui

Abstract This paper discusses the theoretical issues related to the development of prehistoric civilizations in the Xiyu, pointing out that the development of prehistoric civilizations in this region evolved through the constant influence of ancient civilization centers from the surrounding areas, while at the same time being greatly constrained by environmental factors. The main characteristic of the civilization here is the long-term coexistence and mutual learning of agricultural, and animal husbandry and nomadic cultures. The continuous southward and eastward movement of nomadic cultures on the steppe was a major factor in the spread of culture and the migration of peoples on a large scale, while the Xinjiang region served as a bridge and link between the ancient civilizations of the East and the West.

Keyword The region of Xiyu · Prehistoric civilizations · Theoretical issues

8.1 Basic Conditions for the Formation of Prehistoric Civilizations in the Xiyu Region

The Xiyu (西域) region in this paper is a broad area, stretching from the Caspian Sea in the west to the Hangai Mountains in Mongolia and the western part of the Qilian Mountain in China, and from the Kopetdag Mountain, Hindu Kush Mountain, Pamir and Kunlun Mountains in the south to the Altai Mountain, the western Sayan Ridge and northern Kazakhstan in the north, which is also known as the Central Asian region. The Xinjiang region of China is located in what is traditionally known as the eastern part of the Xiyu, or the eastern part of Central Asia.

The famous Soviet scholar B. M. Masson, when evaluating the historical status of the Central Asian civilizations, has pointed out that in the course of studying the ancient history of Central Asia, two basic cultural components of this regional

---

T. Shui (✉)
School of History, Nanjing University, Nanjing, China
e-mail: shuitaonj@126.com

© SDX Joint Publishing 2023
X. Li (ed.), *Major Archaeological Discoveries Along the Chinese Silk Road*,
Silk Road Research Series, https://doi.org/10.1007/978-981-99-0659-8_9

ancient history are evident: the Iranian-Mesopotamian cultural factor and the Kazakh-Siberian cultural element.[1] Between the two, it should be admitted that the role of West Asian civilizations was more important as the earliest known types of cultures based on agriculture and livestock breeding originated in West Asia, such as the Natufian Culture in Palestine and Syria, dating from around 10,000–8000 B.C.; the Karim-Shahi'r Site in northern Iraq, dating from around 9000–8000 B.C.; and the Jericho Site in Jordan, dating from around 9000–8000 B.C. These early cultural developments resulted in the formation of a series of agricultural societies in the southwest parts of the West and Central Asia during the subsequent period, from around the 7th to the 5th millennium B.C. As this development process evolved, the agricultural societies diverged from the hunters, fishermen and gatherers, creating the first social division of labor. As a result, an imbalance in the cultural and historical development of the various regions emerged in the region of Xiyu, forming a cultural region in the southwest part of the Xiyu with a predominantly agricultural economy, and a cultural region in the northwest Xiyu characterized by hunting, gathering, herding and nomadism. Masson suggests that a number of factors contributed to the emergence of an ancient sedentary agricultural culture in the piedmont zone of the Kopetdag Mountains, including the abundant presence of wild graminaceous plants, and numerous wild animals that could be domesticated as domestic animals; the ecological conditions was conducive to the development of primitive irrigated agriculture; and close links with the highly developed cultures of Iraq and Iran at the time also contributed to the formation of agricultural societies in the region of Xiyu.

In the southwest Xiyu region, the cultural influence of the West Asian can be seen in all stages of cultural development, from the early Djietun culture to the later Namazga culture and Yaz cultures, including the two major urbanization processes. It can therefore be said that the cultural processes in the southwest Xiyu region reflect the influence of the civilizations of the West Asian on the East cultures.

For the southeast Xiyu region, the influence of ancient Indian civilization should also be considered. In places such as Afghanistan and southern Tajikistan, this influence from the direction of India was clearly important for the development of cultures in this region after the Bronze Age. However, the early Indian civilization is relatively more recent than that of the Iranian plateau. It is therefore likely that the transition from a foraging to a productive economy in Afghanistan and northwest India was facilitated by the migration of tribes from the Iranian plateau to the East, as Masson and other scholars speculated.

In the northwest Xiyu region, from the Paleolithic onwards, the widespread Neanderthal and later Cro-Magnon populations had arrived in the vast steppe areas of Central Asia. The large number of finds of Mousterian cultural remains demonstrates the extensive links between this region and European culture. The widespread distribution of the Andronovo and Scythian cultures during the Bronze Age and Early Iron Age is another indication of the region's long-standing cultural ties with Eastern Europe, the steppes of Southern Russia and the Black Sea coast. It can therefore be

---

[1] B. M. Masson; translated by Jin Ye: "The Historical Status of Central Asian Civilization", in Archaeological Reference, 1980, No. 3–4, Heritage Press, pp. 1–24.

argued that for this region, the pastoral and nomadic cultures from the West, in its expansion to the East, always had the northwest part of the Xiyu region as its broadest arena of activity. This influence from the West was the most important driving force of the region's cultural development. Later, as the nomads became stronger, this influence was extended to the southwest and southeast regions of the Xiyu.

In the Xinjiang area of China, which is the East part of Xiyu region, in addition to this cultural tradition from the West, there is also the influence of the cultural tradition from the Central Plains to its East. Although few cultural remains have been found in Xinjiang that are dated back to an earlier period, their cultural features are unclear. However, at least from the Bronze Age onwards, such cultural elements from the Central Plains have been presented in the eastern part of Xinjiang and gradually entered the Tarim Basin.

The Khwarezmia region, in the heart of the Xiyu region, evolved too slowly, as it did not have direct cultural interactions with the surrounding centers of ancient civilization. So, it failed to becoming a center of cultural development in the Xiyu region. Throughout the Neolithic Age, it is clear that the cultural development of the area evolved gradually in line with that of the southwest Kopet-Dag Range's piedmont zone. Scholars such as Masson have argued that it was these interactions with the south Xiyu regions and their influence that facilitated of the transition of the northern tribes to a new economic form to a considerable extent. By the Late Bronze Age, however, cultural development here was strongly influenced by nomadic cultures from the northwest Xiyu region by contrast.

In general terms, therefore, the basic driving force behind the emergence and development of prehistoric civilizations in the Xiyu region was the constant influence of other developed centers of ancient civilization in the vicinity, a region which was not equipped to become a center of civilization in its own right. This situation is quite different from the civilizational processes found in West Asia and the Central Plains of China, where civilizations were formed and developed independently under local conditions.

8.2 Interaction Between Agricultural Culture and Nomadic Culture Zones

The cultural development paths of the southwest and northwest Xiyu can be simply summarized as an agricultural cultural path and a nomadic cultural path, which coexisted and developed in parallel. The earliest sedentary agricultural culture emerged in the front area of Kopet-Dag Range, which contributed to the emergence and long-term stable development of the agricultural economy of the entire southwestern region. The prosperity of this agricultural economy was a prerequisite for the rise of the urban economy in the region.

Since the beginning of the Bronze Age, the southwestern region of the Xiyu gradually entered the stage of urbanization, so some scholars attribute the nature of ancient Central Asian civilization to the urban civilization system.[2] Historians of the classical era called Daxia (Bactria) the land of a thousand cities. According to Litvinsky and other scholars, certain structures and layouts of the large buildings of Daxia during the Achaemenid dynasty were the basis for the development of the later Kushan period architecture and, under certain conditions, even for the development of medieval architecture. From the archaeological findings, the formation and development of these cities went through different stages of development, such as agricultural settlements, central settlements, early castles and urban economies, fortified cities and central cities. Therefore, in the southwestern region of the Xiyu, urbanization was the inevitable end of the development of agricultural economy. At the same time, urbanization was also the result of the complex ethnic relations, nation relations, politics and religion in this region.

In the northwestern region of the Xiyu, the subsistence evolved from the initial hunting and gathering to the animal husbandry and nomadic economy, and the stable development of this economic has been maintained in the long-term historical process. At the same time, these nomads played a great role in the formation of the economy, culture and ethnicity of the ancient Central Asian peoples. For example, scholars such as Litvinsky believe that the Saka were a fundamental component in the formation of the Pamir tribes and that they also played a significant role in the formation of other Central Asian tribes. The Saka also made a significant contribution to Central Asian art (especially the "Animal styles"), material culture and the military. The Saka and their culture have played an important role in the history of India, Xinjiang, China, Afghanistan, Iran and the entire Middle East. Saka's immigrants and slaves were also involved in building the economic base of the Achaemenid dynasty, and Saka's culture was one of the most important components of ancient eastern culture.

In Xinjiang, the eastern part of the Xiyu, there were also cultural types represented by the agricultural economy in the oasis and the animal husbandry and nomadic economy in the mountainous and plateau area, which coexisted for a long time throughout the Bronze Age. It was only in the second half of the 1st millennium B.C. that the phenomenon of different economic components coexisting in the same cultural remains began to appear. For the development of prehistoric civilization in the Xiyu, on the one hand, there is a coexistence of these two subsistence strategies. On the other hand, it should also be noted that the area where these two economic worked often changed. From the Neolithic period onwards, influenced by the agricultural culture of the piedmont area of the Kopet-Dag Range, a simple semi-agricultural, semi-hunting and fishing economy began to emerge in the Khwaremia region, and the agricultural culture gradually expanded to the northeast, and the representative cultural remains of this period, the Kelteminar culture, have been found in a wide distribution. At the latest, during the Bronze Age, many oases in Xinjiang in the eastern part of the Xiyu also had an agricultural economy. It is not clear whether

---

[2] Б. A. Litvinsky, translated by Mo Runxian, "Studies on the History and Cultural History of Ancient Central Asia by Soviet Scholars from 1967 to 1977", in Archaeological Reference Materials, 1980, No. 3–4, Antiquities Press, pp. 64–96.

the early agricultural techniques in the eastern part of the Xiyu originated directly from the southwestern Xiyu, since an irrigated agricultural technique was developed in the piedmont zone of Kopet-Dag Range, where crops such as barley, wheat and pea were grown. In the eastern part of the Xiyu, such as Gansu and Qinghai and its eastern areas, the dry farming is the mainly method for crops, such as millet and cruciferous oilseed rape. In some of the early cultural remains in eastern Xinjiang, barley and wheat were the main crops grown, while cereals and sorghum were also found.[3] However, no clear evidence of irrigated agriculture seems to have been found. The findings from eastern Xinjiang suggest that by the Bronze Age, the agricultural economy in Xinjiang had common elements of both cultural traditions, which is consistent with the characteristics reflected in the other components of these cultural remains. We can assume that barley and wheat cultivation techniques were introduced to Xinjiang from the West at an earlier stage.

In the Khwaremia region, the development of the Kelteminar culture never resulted in the formation of large sedentary agricultural settlements, nor in the emergence of an urban economic system developed from agricultural settlements. The reason for this is that the climatic and environmental conditions in the region were different from those in the southwest Xiyu, and the distance from the civilizational centers of Western Asia made it obvious that the degree of acceptance of their influence was greatly diminished. Another important aspect is the strong cultural tradition of hunting, gathering, animal husbandry and nomadic economy that has always existed here. This tradition not only retarded the development of the local agricultural economy, but also, from the Bronze Age onwards, due to the growing strength of nomadic tribes, different tribes of nomads entered the agro-cultural zone from different directions, and in the southern part of Turkmenistan, from the second half of the second millennium B.C., steppe tribes began to penetrate strongly into the areas where settled agricultural tribes were distributed. This migration of the steppe population led to significant changes in the material and spiritual culture, especially in the economy and way of life, of the original population groups of this region. During this period, local animal husbandry developed faster, while agriculture developed more slowly. Discussing the process of the spread of the Andronovo culture, Masson points out that this culture developed in two directions: in irrigated agricultural areas, for example, in the lower Amu Darya zone, where settled agricultural oases were formed on the basis of this culture; and in steppe and semi-desert areas, where early nomads were formed (only these nomads were, to some extent, not the Andronovo tribe itself). Analyzing this situation, Litvinsky points out that as a result of all this, and probably also some physical geography, certain rather large tribal groups began to move eastward from the eastern edge of the distribution area of agricultural tribes. A large part of these tribes entered the river basin—the area along with the tributaries of the rivers Pyandzh and Amu Darya, while others migrated southward into Afghanistan. During the initial and subsequent contacts, the "steppe herders" who were integrated into the settled farming population acquired the material culture of

---

[3] Zhang Cheng'an: "An analysis of agricultural production in Hami during the Bronze Age", in Xinjiang Cultural Relics, No. 4, 1997.

the farming population. At the same time, they exerted their own influence on the burial practices of the farming areas, and not only that, but the Aryan language of the foreign steppe herders was also widely spread among the farming people.[4]

Therefore, when summarizing the characteristics of the prehistoric civilization of the Xiyu, Litvinsky believes that the entry of pastoralists into the agricultural oasis and their gradual transformation from foreigners into an integral part of the oasis culture is an important feature of the prehistoric civilization of the Xiyu. Moreover, because of these inextricable ties between the agricultural and nomadic cultural areas, the most dynamic economic, cultural, ethnic and social interactions took place at the intersection of these two regions. The cities of the northern coast of the Black Sea, the Scythian region, the cities of Central Asia, and the steppes and mountains of Central Asia and Kazakhstan occupied by nomadic herders belong to this type of intersection.[5]

8.3 The Influence of Environmental Factors on the Development of Prehistoric Civilization in the Xiyu

The Xiyu is far from the sea, with mountains and deserts all over the territory. Generally speaking, such environmental conditions were very difficult for human survival. The Soviet scholar Ranov, V. A. has discussed the problem of human settlement in the alpine regions of Asia during the Stone Age.[6] What forced the primitive tribes to leave the rich valleys with low terrain, suitable for survival and convenient transportation, and make such dangerous trips to the mountainous area? In addition to the explanation of hunting tribes migrating with herds of animals and the differentiation of tribes arising from the development of social organization, one of the most important reasons lies in the natural ecological aspects.

According to the Soviet scholar Л. Ф. Sidorov, in the early Pleistocene, the Pamir Plateau had not yet risen to its present height, and in the intermountainous areas, on the riverbanks, there was a wide range of forests, and on the slopes, pine forests and other trees were widely distributed. The vegetation of the plateau had not yet reached its present form until the historical period, accordingly, at least during the first half

---

[4] Б. А. Litvinsky, translated by Mo Runxian, "Archaeological Discoveries in Soviet Tajikistan and Some Problems in the Ancient History of Central Asia", in Archaeological Reference Materials, 1980, No. 3–4, Cultural Relics Publishing House, pp. 25–63.

[5] Studies on the History and Cultural History of Ancient Central Asia by Soviet Scholars, 1967–1977, pp. 64–96.

[6] Ranov, V. A., translated by Liu Shuyong, "Pamir and Stone Age Human Settlement in the Alpine Regions of Asia", in Archaeological Reference, 1980, 3–4, pp. 97–133. In: Archaeological Reference, 1980, No. 3–4, pp. 97–133.

of the Pleistocene, the altitude of the region was low, and the climate was mild and humid.[7]

A characteristic feature of the ecological conditions in the high mountain regions of the Xiyu is the existence of different geomorphological forms and flora and fauna in these mountain systems, from the foot of the mountains upwards in the order of plains, piedmont zones and large low-lying basins, such as Fergana then severely incised high mountain zones, at altitudes of 500–4000 m above sea level, as well as the elevated, weakly incised valleys a lower deposits of high mountain areas, such as the hillside of the Tianshan, and Pamir Plateau and the Ridge denudation, i.e., the area of modern glacial action, above 4500 m above sea level. From a macroscopic point of view, the entry of primitive tribes into these high mountain areas was a gradual process that took a long time. Throughout the Paleolithic, primitive people not only lived in the mountainous areas of the Xiyu during the interglacial period, but also, they used to live under even harsher conditions, i.e., the period of intensified glaciation in the mountains. In fact, the mountainous areas of Xiyu that did not experience overlying continental glaciation in the Quaternary can be divided into two zones, the mountainous areas that retain the remains of glaciation and the unglaciated zones, which include all large basins and valleys below 2000 m in elevation. According to Ranov's research, all reliable Paleolithic remains of the present day are distributed in the unglaciated zone until the end of the Pleistocene, when human activity into the high mountain regions of the Xiyu intensified.

All the most important archaeological discoveries in the Xiyu are concentrated in piedmont areas, or large mountain basins and valleys, because this piedmont environment provided the richest and most diverse plant and animal resources for early hunting, gathering, fishing and other economic types, and most typical areas is the Kopet-Dag Range. When people mastered the techniques of sedentary agriculture, the rivers in front the mountain became an essential source of water for irrigation. It was in the piedmont area that people first learned irrigation agriculture and then developed the deltas downstream of the rivers, as reflected in the process of cultural development from Anau and Namazga-Tepe to the site of Geoksiur in the TedZhen River delta. The concentration of the largest number of primitive tribes and populations in the piedmont zone soon led to problems with the resources of this area, and we see that a large number of very important sites, such as Namazga-Tepe, Altyn-Tepe and Geoksyur, suffered the same fate of being abandoned after a period of prosperity. The reasons for the abandonment of individual sites may vary, such as the diversion of rivers, the desertification of the land, the pressure of the population, etc. As a general phenomenon, many scholars have noted that in the first half of the second millennium B.C., two ancient cultural centers in the southwestern part of the Xiyu, Namazga-Tepe and Altyn-Tepe, began to be abandoned at the same time, and the decline of the culture of this period, represented by the Namazga-Tepe VI culture, is obvious. Almost at the same time, the sites of Tepe Hissar in northern Iran were also uninhabited. The site of Mundigak in southern Afghanistan was reduced

---

[7] Л. Ф. Sirodov: "Development of Pamir vegetation after the Ice Age" (in Russian), in Journal of Botany, 1963, vol. 48, no. 5. The Historical Status of Civilizations in Central Asia, pp. 1–24.

to rubble. In some places in the south, many oases were deserted, and urban civilizations in India, such as Sindh and Punjab, declined. Some scholars have suggested that the decline of ancient agricultural culture in southern Turkmenistan was related to the increased role of animal husbandry, when some farmers switched to primarily pastoral activities.[8] However, this explication does not explain why the role of animal husbandry suddenly continued to increase on such a large scale. We believe that the answer to this change should be sought in terms of environmental change.

From the beginning of this century to modern times, there have been various theories trying to explain the relationship between the desertification process and environmental changes in various parts of the Xiyu starting from the beginning of the second millennium B.C. However, this understanding has not been deepened due to the lack of sufficient relevant information. In recent years, there have been many new developments in the study of Holocene climate change, and Chinese scholars have found that there was a significant cold period climatic effect in Western China starting around 2000 B.C,[9] which had a significant impact on the development of Bronze Age culture in Western China.[10] This cold period also manifested itself in most parts of the Xiyu. Some scholars believe that during the period of global warming, most parts of the Xiyu were in a dry environment under anticyclonic control, and the water level of the Caspian Sea continued to decline until its historical low between 4000 and 2000 B.C.[11] When the cold period started, the climatic conditions in the Xiyu improved, and the degree of humidity increased considerably. For tribes engaged in sedentary agriculture, the increase in winter precipitation was not necessarily a good thing, but for nomadic tribes, the expansion of pasture areas allowed them to move southward long distances into many former agricultural areas. In some centers of sedentary agriculture, such as Altyndepe, long-term prosperity has led to rapid population growth, and the consumption and destruction of water resources and vegetation may lead to environmental degradation. Therefore, on the one hand, the nomadic economy was given the opportunity to develop greatly, and on the other hand, the agricultural economy was faced with many problems in its development, and at this time, some farmers had to turn to animal husbandry, which further strengthened the animal husbandry economic component in the agricultural region. Of course, the reasons for the large-scale ethnic migration must be very complex and cannot be put simply. In other words, the role of environmental changes may be one of the important conditions, but the more profound reasons may come from the tendency of tribal differentiation within the social organization, etc.

---

[8] Shi Yafeng et al. "Climate and environment in China during the heyday of the Holocene Warm Period", in Science of China (Series B), vol. 23, no. 8, 1993.

[9] Shui Tao: "Study on the cultural structure and economic pattern of the Bronze Age in Gansu and Qinghai", Papers on the Bronze Age Archaeology of Northwest China, Science Press, 2002.

[10] H. H. Lamb, Translated by Y. C. Wang, Y. S. Yao, and A. J. Sun, Climate Change and Prospects, Meteorological Press, 1987, pp. 64–65.

[11] V. M. Masson and T. P. Kiiatkina: Man at Dawn of Civilization, The Bronze Age Civilization of Central Asia -Recent Soviet Discoveries, Amonk, New York, 1981, pp. 108–109.

8.4 The Relationship Between the Prehistoric Civilizations of the Xiyu and Other Regions

In examining the conditions for the emergence of prehistoric civilizations in the Xiyu, we note the close ties that existed between the Xiyu and the early civilizations of Western Asia and Mesopotamia. These connections are manifested in many cultural features, such as irrigated agricultural techniques, small adobe buildings, the art of planning and layout of large cities and temple buildings, small statues of goddesses, small animal statues, metal smelting techniques, the art of modeling seals and cylinder seal, and so on. These connections are often due to the entry of new tribal groups from northern Iran into the southwestern or southeastern regions of the Xiyu, who brought new cultural elements to these regions and changed the course of cultural development in these areas.

When it comes to the issue of tribal migration, the most important event is the so-called Aryan migration. Many scholars believe that the Aryans migrated into eastern Iran and India through the territory of Central Asia. Others believe that it was through the Caucasus. According to Litvinsky, neither the "Central Asian theory" nor the "Caucasian theory" can solve all the practical problems in isolation. The real process may be much more complex, including a series of migrations, some through the Caucasus and some through Central Asia. Moreover, the Aryan language may have spread in southern Central Asia as early as the middle of the second millennium BCE. When analyzing these events, it is important to note that the Andronovo tribe, which most likely spoke Aryan languages in the West, had a very similar cultural representation to Timber-chambered Tomb. In this regard, the research of the famous Russian scholar E. E. Kuzmina, using archaeological, linguistic, documentary and other materials, has clarified such issues as the cultural commonality of the Andronovo culture in Kazakhstan with the ancient Indo-Aryan-speaking population of South Asia.[12] In the Late Bronze Age, Central Asia was undoubtedly the place of migration of some Aryan tribes. These Aryan tribes, on the one hand, became the main component of the later Central Asian peoples, and on the other hand, they spread the Aryan language farther into eastern Iran, Afghanistan, and India. At the same time, several other migrations from western and southwestern Iran also reached these regions.[13]

Another issue worth studying is the spread of Scythian art to the East. From the discovered archaeological and cultural remains, the Sakas are found in the north-western, northeastern and southeastern parts of the Xiyu, especially in the central Tianshan and Pamir regions, where the distribution is very dense. In the Altai Mountains and the Yenisei River valley, cultural remains with a strong Scythian artistic style can also be found. At the same time, we can say that the influence of Scythian art has reached as far as Mongolia and the northern China. The Scythian art style has had a profound influence on the later steppe culture in Xiyu, as we can see from the

---

[12] Е. Е. Кузьмина, Откудапришпииндоарии, Москва:РоссийскаяАкадемияНаук, 1994.

[13] Archaeological Discoveries in Tajikistan during the Soviet Period and Some Problems in the Ancient History of Central Asia", pp. 25–63.

Pazyryk burial, the Oxus Treasure, the Tillya Tepe gold treasure and other discoveries. The reason why Scythian art spread widely in the Xiyu is that the northwestern region of the Xiyu has always had close cultural contact and tribal interaction with the Black Sea region and the West Ural Mountains, and the two regions have a common cultural tradition. Therefore, when the Scythian tribes flourished in the Black Sea, the northwestern region of Xiyu soon became a new ideal home for the Serbs. When the ancient Indo-European peoples entered the area around the Tarim Basin in Xinjiang is also an important academic hot issue. In recent years, many ancient specimens of ancient corpses have been found in Xinjiang, such as the mummies found in Tiebanhe and Xiaohe in the lower reaches of the Kongque River; the mummies found in Wubu in Hami; the mummies found in Zhahongluke in Qiemo; and the mummies found in Subeixi in Shanshan. Although the age of the cultural remains represented by these discoveries varies, it is noteworthy that most of these mummies have the characteristics of Caucasoid in terms of physical trait. Therefore, many scholars have attempted to link these findings to the Indo-European peoples, such as the Tocharians, who were historically active around the Tarim Basin.[14] The discussion in this area reached a climax with the international conference "Bronze Age and Early Iron Age Peoples of Eastern Central Asia" held at the University of Pennsylvania in April 1996.[15] Although scholars from different countries differ in their views on some issues, there is a consensus that the group of people represented by these mummies around 2000–1000 B.C. is very likely to have some origin with the Tocharians and Tocharians languages. It is worth mentioning that researchers in many countries are not only relying on the findings of historical evidence, anthropology, archaeology, comparative linguistics, mythology, etc., but some scholars have started to look for new breakthroughs and discoveries from the perspective of genetics and molecular archaeology, trying to prove the correlation between genetic and linguistic data, and thus linking the ethnic-linguistic and cultural characteristics.[16]

In discussing the issue of the documentation of the Tocharians people, some scholars believe that the Yuezhi is one of the Tocharians. Their initial residence is not in the traditional view of Gansu Dunhuang to the western part of the Qilian Mountains but should be in the eastern part of the Tianshan Mountains in Xinjiang, Bogda Mountain, Balikun Mountain to the eastern part of the Altai Mountains between the grassland area.[17] According to this view, it is possible to link the cultural remains

---

[14] For a wide range of articles on the subject, see the special issue of The Journal of Indo-European Studies, Vol. 23, No. 3–4, Fall/Winter 1995.

[15] Xu Wengkan, "A Review of the International Symposium on "Bronze and Early Iron Age Peoples in Eastern Central Asia", in The Western Regions Studies, No. 3, 1996.

[16] Francalacci, Paolo DNA Analysis of Ancient Corpses from Xinjiang, The Journal of Indo-European Studies, Vol. 23, No. 3 & 4, Fall/Winter 1995, pp. 385–398. Weng Zili, Yuan Yida, and Du Ruofu, "Analysis ofthe genetic structure of Chinese populations", in Journal of Anthropology, vol. 8, no. 3 (1989), pp. 261–268.

[17] Lin Meicun: "Qilian and Kunlun", in Dunhuang Research, 1994, no. 6; Lin Meicun: "The Tocharrians and the Dragon Tribe", in Western Studies, 1997, no. 1; Lin Meicun: "An Examination of the Tuhuolian Deities", in Studies in Sinology, vol. (1998, no. 1); Lin Meicun: "A Study of the Tocharrians Deities", in Studies in National Studies, vol. 5, Peking University Press, 1998, pp. 1–26.

found in the eastern part of Xinjiang, which contain European types, with those of the Tocharians-Yuezhi. Of course, the problem has not been solved in full, some scholars noted that in the early grotto wall paintings throughout Xinjiang, there is a part of the preservation of the image of the Tocharians people, some of which are dark-eyed black people.[18] These people are not identical to the mummies of the Caucasian found in eastern Xinjiang, which are characterized by blond hair, blue eyes, and light skin. Therefore, the distribution and migration of early Indo-European peoples in Xinjiang have become complicated over time, and research on these issues is still in the exploratory stage.

Xinjiang, located in the eastern part of the Xiyu, not only received cultural influences from the West and the East, but also, in many cases, served as a bridge and link between the West and the East. There are many discoveries about the origins of metallurgy, and the West Asian region is the most important center. Thus, some scholars have linked early bronze and iron tools from central China to discoveries in Western or Central Asia when exploring their origins.[19] In fact, since there is no Bronze Age cultural remains earlier than 2000 B.C. have been identified in Xinjiang, it is difficult to say how this diffusion arose and how it took place. Perhaps, as far as the present material shows, metallurgy may have spread from West to East along the steppe zone in the northern part of the Xiyu, and in the Minusinsk Basin the Karasuk culture was very closely linked to the Shang culture of China, and this link must have started at an earlier date. The Andronovo culture, which was widespread in most parts of the Xiyu, on the one hand, established the connection between the northwestern part and the southwestern Xiyu, and on the other hand, it was possible to spread to the East with various technological elements of steppe culture, including horseback riding, carriage, metallurgy, nomadic arts, etc. Before the opening of the Silk Road, the role played by the nomadic culture of the steppe in bridging the cultural ties between the West and the East was much greater than the role played by the agricultural peoples distributed in a relatively isolated oasis environment, and this should not be overlooked. Each technological tradition of agricultural peoples is developed on the basis of long-term adaptation to local environmental conditions, such as the traditional irrigation technology, wheat cultivation technology, adobe construction technology in the desert areas of southwestern Xiyu, the dryland cultivation technology of millet crops, kiln construction technology in the Central Plains of China. Once these traditions were spread out of the special environmental conditions, they do not become cultural factors that have the advantage of spreading outward. In the early years, Anderson and others argued that the Yangshao culture of the Central Plains of China was spread from the West. Now, on the one hand, discoveries in various parts of the Central Plains of China show that the culture of the Central Plains is of local origin. On the other hand, discoveries in Xinjiang and the Xiyu

---

[18] Chen Jian-Wen, "A Re-examination of the Yuezhi tribe", in Shigeng (Institute of History, National Taiwan Normal University), 1995, pp. 49–68.

[19] Louisa G. Fitzgerald-Huber, Qijia and Erlitou: The Question of Contacts with Distant Cultures. Early China 20, 1995, pp. 17–67.Chen Ge: "The Western Regions in the Prehistoric Period", in Yu Taishan, ed: A Complete History of the Western Regions, Zhongzhou Chinese Classics Publishing House (1996), pp. 16–31.

also indicate that throughout the prehistoric period, there were not many cultural ties between the Xiyu and the Central Plains of China, and the role of such ties was not very significant. This situation continued until Zhang Qian's passage to the Xiyu, after which the interaction between China's Central Plains and the Xiyu intensified considerably.

Printed by Libri Plureos GmbH
in Hamburg, Germany